Licensing and Managing Electronic Resources

CHANDOS
INFORMATION PROFESSIONAL SERIES

Series Editor: Ruth Rikowski
(email: Rikowskigr@aol.com)

Chandos' new series of books are aimed at the busy information professional. They have been specially commissioned to provide the reader with an authoritative view of current thinking. They are designed to provide easy-to-read and (most importantly) practical coverage of topics that are of interest to librarians and other information professionals. If you would like a full listing of current and forthcoming titles, please visit our website **www.chandospublishing.com** or contact Hannah Grace-Williams on e-mail info@chandospublishing.com or telephone number +44 (0) 1993 848726.

New authors: we are always pleased to receive ideas for new titles; if you would like to write a book for Chandos, please contact Dr Glyn Jones on e-mail gjones@chandospublishing.com or telephone number +44 (0) 1993 848726.

Bulk orders: some organisations buy a number of copies of our books. If you are interested in doing this, we would be pleased to discuss a discount. Please contact Hannah Grace-Williams on e-mail info@chandospublishing.com or telephone number +44 (0) 1993 848726.

Licensing and Managing Electronic Resources

BECKY ALBITZ

Chandos Publishing

Oxford · England

Chandos Publishing (Oxford) Limited
TBAC Business Centre
Avenue 4
Station Lane
Witney
Oxford OX28 4BN
UK
Tel: +44 (0) 1993 848726 Fax: +44 (0) 1865 884448
E-mail: info@chandospublishing.com
www.chandospublishing.com

First published in Great Britain in 2008

ISBN:
978 1 84334 432 2 (paperback)
978 1 84334 433 9 (hardback)
1 84334 432 7 (paperback)
1 84334 433 5 (hardback)

© R. Albitz, 2008

British Library Cataloguing-in-Publication Data.
A catalogue record for this book is available from the British Library.

Typeset by Domex e-Data Pvt. Ltd.
Printed in the UK and USA.

Contents

List of tables

About the author

Becky Albitz holds the position of electronic resources and copyright librarian at the Pennsylvania State University. She earned her undergraduate degrees in film and English from the University of Rochester, her master's in film from Penn State and her MLS from the University of Pittsburgh; she is working on her doctorate in higher education at Penn State. As a former media librarian at the University of Iowa and New York University, Becky has extensive experience with copyright issues as they pertain to media, and has actively engaged in media and copyright-related organizations within the American Library Association. She is currently chair of the Association of College and Research Libraries Copyright Committee. Her publications on media, licensing and copyright have appeared in a variety of venues, including *portal*, the *Journal of Academic Librarianship*, *The Reference Librarian*, *Collection Development* and *The Acquisitions Librarian*. Becky co-taught the Association of Research Libraries online licensing workshop with Trisha Davis from Ohio State, and has given numerous presentations and workshops on copyright, the Digital Millennium Copyright Act, the Technology, Education, and Copyright Harmonization (TEACH) Act and electronic resource licensing.

The author can be contacted via the publishers.

Acknowledgements

Before I became an electronic resources librarian, I had no background in law or business. I did understand the fundamentals behind copyright law, because, as a media librarian, I had to understand what people could and could not do with the library's video collection. That after only seven years in this position I am able to write a book offering advice to other newly minted electronic resources librarians is due to the help and support given by a number of wonderful colleagues. I will forever be in debt to Bonnie MacEwan, who gave me the opportunity and offered the guidance I needed as a new electronic resources librarian. Trisha Davis had the faith in my abilities to take me on as her ARL online licensing workshop co-instructor. Jim Stemper, Susan Barribeau, Wendy Shelburne and Jaime Jamison all provide me with the laughter and support I need to make it through the tougher negotiations. And I thank the faculty and staff of the Penn State University Libraries, at all locations, who continue to support and encourage me every day.

Above all, I thank Cherry Ekins for her wonderful editing and excellent sense of humor, John Swinton, my father, for his indexing skills and constant, unwavering support, and finally Donna Ferullo for reading a draft of this book and correcting all my legal misunderstandings. I am forever grateful to you all.

List of acronyms

AEA	American Economic Association
CLIR	Council on Library Information Resources
CLOCKSS	controlled LOCKSS
CONFU	Conference on Fair Use
CONTU	National Commission on New Technological Uses of Copyrighted Works
COUNTER	Counting Online Usage of Networked Electronic Resources
DDP	deep discount pricing
DLF	Digital Library Federation
DOI	digital object identifier
ECCO	Eighteenth Century Collections Online
ERL	electronic resources librarian
FAQ	frequently asked questions
FERPA	Family Educational Rights and Privacy Act
FTE	full-time equivalent
ICOLC	International Coalition of Library Consortia
IE	Internet Explorer
IP	internet protocol
ISSN	International Standard Serial Number
LOCKSS	lots of copies keep stuff safe
MARC	machine-readable cataloguing
NISO	National Information Standards Organization
SERU	Shared E-Resource Understanding

SUNY	State University of New York
TEACH	Technology, Education, and Copyright Harmonization Act
UCITA	Uniform Computer Information Transactions Act
WIPO	World Intellectual Property Organization

Legal note

I am not an attorney. Nothing in this book constitutes legal advice. Please contact your institution's legal counsel if you have any questions concerning the legal policies and practices of your library, college, university or state, if appropriate.

Introduction

Ownership versus access has been a long-standing issue in libraries. In the print world, interlibrary loan gives us the opportunity to choose to spend our collection dollars on a book or journal subscription, or to borrow that information from another institution. This option allows us the flexibility to build strong collections in areas that support our institution's research and curricular foci, while still providing access to research-level materials in other areas of faculty and student interest. Those materials we choose to purchase become ours to use as permitted under US copyright law, and to share with other libraries upon request.

In the electronic era, access in particular has taken on a very different meaning. It no longer just refers to borrowing a physical piece from another library. We now use the term to describe information delivery through an electronic product we license, rather than purchase outright. Licensed resources provide our users with a great number of benefits, including remote access, sophisticated searching capabilities and rare content. But because we have to sign a license to offer this access, our ability to use the content is no longer consistent with our rights under copyright law. Our faculty and students do not realize that they may not be permitted to use that electronic journal article as they would the print version, because the license we signed prohibits that use. For librarians, offering access to content rather than purchasing it raises issues concerning use of this material for interlibrary loan and reserves, long-term access and preservation, and content management.

Licensing agreements are not limited to online products only. Our acquisitions departments are now finding contracts accompanying some print books, most frequently those published in business and law. Textbooks in engineering and the sciences now include single-user CD-ROMs with highly restrictive licenses. Some of these contracts require a signature, while others go into effect upon payment of the invoice or with the first use. Some video and DVD distributors are requiring signed license agreements from acquiring libraries, or are imposing usage restrictions that are, again, accepted tacitly when the library pays the bill. And, of course, CD-ROMs and software continue to arrive with shrink-wrap licenses – those that require no signature and whose terms and conditions become valid when the packaging is opened.

Along with this growing number of licensed resources comes the need to manage the licensing process as well as the products themselves. In response, many libraries have established electronic resources librarian positions, while others may assign the licensing, negotiation and management of these products to people already on staff, in addition to their other responsibilities. The person handling some or all activities related to your electronic resources might be the head of serials or acquisitions, a reference librarian or the head of collections. But no matter where in the organization electronic resource oversight lives, these responsibilities are unique within the profession. No other job requires a knowledge of library services, the ability to read and negotiate legal contracts, the skill to maneuver within the world of publishers and information providers, and the technical knowledge to troubleshoot access problems. These positions merge elements of both library and business worlds, and require knowledge taught in library science, masters of business administration and law school programs. Needless to say, opportunities to learn the skills and information necessary to do this job are not widely available. While a few organizations offered in-person and online seminars in the past, these programs have all but disappeared from the continuing education landscape. The goal of this book is to fill that void, and to offer some guidance to those who are new to the arena of licensing and electronic resource management.

Licensing terms and copyright determine how clients and libraries can use information resources. Understanding the relationship between them is a crucial first step in negotiating a license. Copyright is federal law, while contract law is governed by the states. Pre-emption is a doctrine stating that federal law overrides state law, articulated in the Supremacy Clause of the US Constitution (1787). Section VI, Article 2 states:

> This Constitution, and the laws of the United States which shall be made in pursuance thereof; and all treaties made, or which shall be made, under the authority of the United States, shall be the supreme law of the land; and the judges in every state shall be bound thereby, anything in the Constitution or laws of any State to the contrary notwithstanding.

When a conflict exists between state and federal law, the constitution states that federal law will prevail. This is, however, a point of discussion within the legal community, because many courts will uphold contract language even if it is in direct conflict with copyright law. So understanding the difference between what copyright allows us to do with a work and what a contract mandates is necessary to ensure that you can use licensed content in a manner that corresponds to your users' and library's needs.

Once the relationship between copyright law and licensing terms and conditions is understood, the novice license negotiator needs to know the definitions of common legal terms and concepts found in a contract. A generic license will be the foundation of this book, not only to provide definitions of standard licensing terms, but also to offer guidance in making appropriate changes to a contract's language. The changes that will be discussed will fall into two categories: necessary and preferred. Necessary changes are those your state, institution or library mandates for legal or operational reasons. These are considered deal-breakers, meaning a company's willingness to accept these changes will determine whether an institution can move forward with the agreement at all. The contract changes falling in the preferred category may not be legally or operationally necessary but are highly desirable, depending upon a specific institution's needs. Communicating what changes are essential, which are desired and why all are wanted is an important part of the negotiation process.

Selecting and managing individual electronic resources can be as complicated as the licensing process. In some cases the same content may be available from multiple companies. Selecting the most appropriate company might depend upon a company's willingness to negotiate licensing terms and conditions. But other factors, including interface functionality, pricing and access options, can play a part in choosing one company over another. Once a product is selected, you, as the electronic resources librarian, along with your library's collection managers need to review these resources annually, as you do your other subscriptions. You might choose to renegotiate pricing, select a new provider or even cancel the product altogether. These options will be reviewed as part of the management process. Finally, model licensing and other approaches to publisher/librarian agreements, which could reduce or potentially eliminate the need for licenses and negotiations, will be discussed as alternatives to the publisher license.

Licensing, negotiating and managing information resources are responsibilities that are constantly evolving. The intent of this work is to provide a foundation upon which the new electronic resources librarian can build. Since I am not an attorney, and do not have knowledge about individual state and institution requirements, this book should not take the place of consultation with your institution's legal counsel or the administrative officer responsible for purchasing institution-wide. These people understand your university's unique needs and can offer advice to ensure the terms and conditions of these agreements comply with your institution's policies.

Know your copyrights

Copyright might seem an odd topic with which to open a book about electronic resources licensing, negotiation and management, but knowledge of copyright is central to beginning any discussion about licensing. Copyright law, found under Title 17 of the US Code, outlines how we, as consumers of information, are permitted to use material protected under copyright. When we agree to the terms and conditions of use outlined in an information resource's contract, however, we may waive those rights articulated under copyright law. If contract language specifically prohibits certain behaviors, then we may not use the product in that manner, even if those uses are permitted under US copyright law. Even though federal law is supposed to pre-empt state law, in this case the contract would govern our behavior. Therefore it is important that you, as the negotiator of these information resource contracts, understand those rights given to you under copyright law, so you can determine if you need to retain these rights or if contract terms that eliminate some of your copyrights are acceptable.

A brief history of US copyright law

Copyright law in the USA evolved from the Statute of Anne, a British law enacted in 1709. Though named for Queen

Anne, the first copyright law was officially called 'An Act for the Encouragement of Learning, by vesting the Copies of Printed Books in the Authors or purchasers of such Copies, during the Times therein mentioned'. This Act allowed authors to retain the reproduction or copying rights to their own works, rather than having those rights transferred to the printer. Authors maintained their rights for 14 years, after which time others were allowed to reproduce the work without obtaining permission. The US version of the Statute of Anne is found under Article 1, section 8 of the US Constitution, which specifies the powers of the legislative branch of government. A portion of this section states that Congress has the power to 'promote the progress of science and useful arts, by securing for limited times to authors and inventors the exclusive right to their respective writings and discoveries'.

The intent of copyright law, as stated in the constitution, is to provide an incentive to authors and inventors to continue their work. This incentive is the exclusive or monopoly right to do with their own works as they choose. The other critical piece of the language in both the Statute of Anne and US copyright law is that this monopoly is intended to be for a limited time. The intention was never to permit the author or inventor to retain exclusive rights to his or her own work forever, although the period of time copyright is in force has steadily increased from 14 years to the current term of 70 years after the author's death.

While the constitution clearly gave authors and inventors control over their own works, US law did not delineate these rights until Congress passed the Copyright Act of 1976. This Act was the first statutory revision to copyright law since 1909, and the first time the law specifically defined an author's or inventor's rights, materials covered under copyright and a third party's rights in using copyrighted works. Much had changed in the world between 1909 and 1976, and these changes needed to be reflected in the law. Newer technologies, such as television and video, obviously had not been invented in 1909, thus the performance, display and ownership of these and other new forms of expression had to be addressed. International treaties also influenced the 1976 Copyright Act. The USA had participated in the Universal Copyright Convention in 1952 and the Second Protocol of the Universal Copyright Convention in 1971, but Congress had not integrated either convention's terms into US copyright law. The result of the Copyright Act of 1976 is what now is known as Title 17 of the US Code.

After Title 17, in response to the rapid technological changes that occurred during the last two decades of the twentieth century and more recent international agreements, including two World Intellectual Property Organization (WIPO) treaties, Congress once again updated copyright law. The Digital Millennium Copyright Act, passed in 1998, added language to the 1976 Act to address the unique fluidity of digital media.

Title 17

Title 17 of the US Code articulates what rights authors have to their own works, as well as exceptions various constituencies enjoy when making use of copyrighted works. These constituencies include individuals, as well as representatives of libraries and archives. Many of these rights can be either lost or retained when negotiating an electronic product's contract. For this brief overview of copyright, the focus will be on Chapter 1 of Title 17, entitled 'Subject Matter and Scope of Copyright'.[1]

Authors' and inventors' rights

Section 106 of Chapter 1 specifies what rights the author holds to a work that falls under copyright. The section reads:

> Subject to sections 107 through 122, the owner of copyright under this title has the exclusive rights to do and to authorize any of the following:
>
> 1. to reproduce the copyrighted work in copies or phonorecords;
>
> 2. to prepare derivative works based upon the copyrighted work;
>
> 3. to distribute copies or phonorecords of the copyrighted work to the public by sale or other transfer of ownership, or by rental, lease, or lending;
>
> 4. in the case of literary, musical, dramatic, and choreographic works, pantomimes, and motion pictures and other audiovisual works, to perform the copyrighted work publicly;
>
> 5. in the case of literary, musical, dramatic, and choreographic works, pantomimes, and pictorial, graphic, or sculptural works, including the individual images of a motion picture or other audiovisual work, to display the copyrighted work publicly; and
>
> 6. in the case of sound recordings, to perform the copyrighted work publicly by means of a digital audio transmission.

In summary, copyright holders have the right to reproduce, distribute, perform, display or transmit digitally their work, as well as the right to prepare works based on the original.

Although copyright holders may permit others to use their work in any of these ways, they continue to retain their exclusive rights. The information provider, from which you will be licensing some form of digital content, either owns the copyright to the works it is offering or has obtained permission from those who own the copyright to reproduce and distribute this content.

Rights of those using a copyrighted work

Appropriately, copyright holders retain control over the use of their works. The reason for this control is, as mentioned previously, to encourage authors, artists and inventors to continue their work, and enable them perhaps to earn a living doing so. Promoting creativity is how new and exciting works are discovered or created, and such activity benefits society as a whole. But those writing the 1976 Copyright Act understood that people other than the copyright holder should be permitted to use protected works, because the results of use by a non-copyright holder might benefit society as much as the original work. To address this need, sections 107–122 within Title 17 specify limits to the copyright holder's exclusive rights as outlined in section 106.

Section 107 – fair use

Perhaps the least understood limitation to a copyright holder's exclusive rights is contained within this section, which outlines the concept of fair use:

> Notwithstanding the provisions of sections 106 and 106A, the fair use of a copyrighted work, including such use by reproduction in copies or phonorecords or

by any other means specified by that section, for purposes such as criticism, comment, news reporting, teaching (including multiple copies for classroom use), scholarship, or research, is not an infringement of copyright. In determining whether the use made of a work in any particular case is a fair use the factors to be considered shall include –

1. the purpose and character of the use, including whether such use is of a commercial nature or is for nonprofit educational purposes;
2. the nature of the copyrighted work;
3. the amount and substantiality of the portion used in relation to the copyrighted work as a whole; and
4. the effect of the use upon the potential market for or value of the copyrighted work.

The fact that a work is unpublished shall not itself bar a finding of fair use if such finding is made upon consideration of all the above factors.

People in higher education take advantage of fair use every day when they use copyrighted material in their teaching, research and scholarship. Commenting on copyrighted works occurs frequently in academe, and is a critical part of the scholarly inquiry process. Section 107 allows a third party to make use of a copyrighted work for such purposes. If a copyright holder questions the legality of a use, and the person using the copyrighted work can justify and defend their use based upon the four factors outlined above, then their use would be considered a fair use.

A misconception among those in higher education is that every use they make of copyrighted material is a fair use, because their work is (usually) for non-profit educational and research purposes. But this is not the case, as non-profit educational use is only one of the four factors considered in a fair use determination. All four factors listed in this section are intended to act as measures against which a use is assessed. The easiest way to understand how a judge decides a fair use case is to imagine the use of a copyrighted work falling on one of two sides of a scale – one side is in favor of fair use, and the other is against. After analyzing a use based upon all four factors, the scale will tip either in favor of a fair use ruling or against it. A judge will ultimately determine the validity of a fair use claim.

- *Purpose of use.* The first of these four factors relates to the purpose of the use of the copyrighted work. If the use is for non-profit educational reasons, that would strongly support a fair use defense. Using a copyrighted work for commercial purposes, however, would not support fair use, since the copyright holder would be deprived of income generated from the use of his or her personal creative efforts. Some uses might fall between these two extremes – for example, use of a copyrighted work in a publication which generates income but is intended for educational use. These and other less clear-cut examples are evaluated on a case-by-case basis.

- *Nature of the work.* The second factor focuses on the copyrighted work itself. What kind of work is it? The work may be fiction or non-fiction, a work of art, published or unpublished. Notice that facts are not included in the list of options. Facts are not copyrightable, because a work must have an element of originality to be copyrighted. By definition, facts do not meet this test. Based on this premise, utilization of a non-fiction work, or a work containing a great deal of factual information, would lean more toward a fair use determination, while a work of fiction or a painting would receive more protection under the law. The level of copyright protection also differs between those works that have been published and those that are unpublished. The act of publication indicates that the copyright holder wants to have his or her work available for others to read, view and use, within the parameters copyright law establishes. The same cannot be said for personal letters, a diary or even a private e-mail, because the writer never intended this type of work to be disseminated widely; thus using a published work is more easily defensible under fair use than using an unpublished work. But, as the section states explicitly, use of an unpublished work might be considered a fair use, depending upon the other three factors.

- *Amount and substantiality of use.* The third factor raises the same question consistently from those who want to use a copyrighted work, and want to do so within the boundaries of the law: how much is too much? Copyright law does not provide an answer to this question. The ambiguous term 'reasonable' is used when discussing the volume of material one can use. Is copying 50 per cent of a work reasonable? Most likely a court would say that 50 per cent is too much, but perhaps 5 per cent is reasonable. The answer would depend on the work being used and the nature of the use.

   In an effort to provide guidance in defining what 'reasonable' is, representatives from the entertainment industry, educational institutions, libraries and the publishing industry gathered at the Conference on Fair Use (CONFU). The resulting guidelines, negotiated in 1996, specified how much of a book, song or movie could be reproduced and displayed in a multimedia work produced for educational purposes and still be considered a fair use. A brief summary of the CONFU multimedia guidelines appears in Appendix II. A number of organizations do not support the results of the conference, including the American Library Association, because the guidelines are considered too restrictive. Others consider the CONFU guidelines to be a 'safe harbor', meaning that if the amount used is within the limits specified, then the user will be protected from legal action under fair use. As of this writing, no one knows if the courts would concur with this position, because no case has been brought against someone who has cited the CONFU guidelines as a defense. (A note: these guidelines are not the law – they are merely suggestions that may be followed or not, as the user deems appropriate.)

The other part of the third factor does not refer to the amount of the original work used, but to the substantiality or importance of the material to the value of the work as a whole. An example of a court case that helps establish the parameters of this factor is *Harper & Row v. Nation Enterprises* (1985). Harper & Row, publisher of *A Time to Heal: The Autobiography of Gerald R. Ford*, had been granted first serial publication rights to this title, along with the right to publish the work in its entirety. The publishers of *Time* magazine purchased the serial rights to the book, which allowed them to publish excerpts prior to the release of the book. A publisher at *The Nation*, a rival magazine, obtained an unauthorized copy of the book manuscript, and chose to publish an article featuring segments of the work prior to *Time*'s scheduled article. *The Nation*'s article contained only 400 words taken directly from the 454-page manuscript, but Harper & Row sued, stating that those 400 words were critical to the value of the book. The Supreme Court, which eventually heard this case, agreed. In its ruling the court acknowledged that the portion of the work copied was very small, but because these 400 words, which centered on Ford's decision to pardon Richard Nixon, were at the heart of the work, it ruled in Harper & Row's favor.

- *Effect on the market.* Finally, the fourth factor focuses on whether the use of the work jeopardizes its commercial value in the marketplace. For many copyright holders this is the most important factor of the four, as the monetary return on a copyrighted work may be their primary source of income or an incentive to continue practicing their craft. Entertainment industry executives are particularly concerned about potential income loss, because the perpetuation of the television and movie industries relies on the willingness of others to pay to consume their products. They see any non-authorized use of their content as decreasing its commercial value, regardless of how the other three factors are weighed. The court case described above provides a specific example of how the fourth factor may be considered. As a result of *The Nation* article's appearance, *Time*'s owners cancelled their agreement with Harper & Row, did not publish the planned article and did not pay the remaining $12,500 they owed for the exclusive serial rights to Ford's autobiography. Harper & Row could prove to the Supreme Court that *The Nation*'s actions had a direct effect upon the market value of the work.

Libraries also rely on the four factors of fair use to provide reserve reading services for their faculty and students. Print reserves have been a library staple for years, but recently publishers have become increasingly concerned about the growth in electronic reserve readings, because they are seeing more digitization of print works but are not seeing the kinds of royalties they expect. In order to offer electronic reserves, librarians scan print articles and book chapters, creating digital versions from the analog. Publishers do not believe that librarians, generally speaking, are paying the appropriate amount to digitize their works, while librarians believe their use of copyrighted material in offering electronic course reserves falls under fair use, as it did when reserve readings were still provided in print only. A great deal of disagreement exists between the library and publishing communities on this topic, as exhibited by a series of letters the American Association of Publishers has delivered to libraries over the past few years, threatening lawsuits for copyright infringement based upon the libraries' electronic reserve services.

As mentioned previously, if fair use is claimed as a defense, then the court will examine how the copyrighted work was used, and weigh this use against each of the four factors outlined above. If, in the judge's opinion, the comparison of the use against the four factors results in an evaluation that leans toward fair use, the defendant will prevail. As each case is considered, the resulting judgment establishes legal precedents, helping to clarify what fair use really means.

What does this discussion about fair use have to do with licensing? Material within licensed databases is copyrighted, and thus those authorized to access the material could use it in a variety of ways under the fair use provision of the copyright law. Faculty members could make multiple copies from these resources for classroom distribution. Students could quote from these databases without explicit permission. Reasonable portions could be incorporated into conference presentations or displays. Unfortunately, if a license prohibits the use of materials contained within an information resource as permitted under section 107, then the flexibility fair use offers is lost.

Rights of libraries and archives

Section 108 articulates the rights libraries and archives have to reproduce copyrighted works, allowing librarians and archivists to preserve collections and offer services such as interlibrary loan and content preservation. When Title 17 was written in 1976, published information was available primarily in print. Now, however, with the proliferation of electronic information sources and the cancellation of print journal subscriptions in favor of electronic titles, concerns about the continued relevance and applicability of section 108 have arisen. As of this writing, the Library of Congress has formed a Section 108 Study Group, consisting of lawyers, publishers, librarians and academics, to make recommendations to update this section. Because no report has been made public, and the Library of Congress has not yet made any recommendations to modernize section 108, librarians will continue to interpret and apply this section's language much as they have in the past.

Library copying

The first portion of section 108 permits a library or archive employee to make a copy of a work. Paragraph 108(a) states:

> (a) Except as otherwise provided in this title and notwithstanding the provisions of section 106, it is not an infringement of copyright for a library or archives, or any of its employees acting within the scope of their employment, to reproduce no more than one copy or phonorecord of a work, except as provided in subsections (b) and (c), or to distribute such copy or phonorecord, under the conditions specified by this section, if –

1. the reproduction or distribution is made without any purpose of direct or indirect commercial advantage;

2. the collections of the library or archives are (i) open to the public, or (ii) available not only to researchers affiliated with the library or archives or with the institution of which it is a part, but also to other persons doing research in a specialized field; and

3. the reproduction or distribution of the work includes a notice of copyright that appears on the copy or phonorecord that is reproduced under the provisions of this section, or includes a legend stating that the work may be protected by copyright if no such notice can be found on the copy or phonorecord that is reproduced under the provisions of this section.

This portion of section 108 states that a library or archive employee can make and distribute a single copy of a copyrighted work, as long as the person making the copy is doing so as part of his or her job. But in order to provide this service, the institution must meet certain criteria. The copies cannot be made for commercial purposes, although cost recovery is permissible. The library or archive also has to be open to the public, or the collections must be made available to researchers. And the copies produced must have a copyright notice – either the one that appears on the original work or a library-constituted notice.

Copies for preservation and replacement

Paragraphs 108(b) and (c) are concerned with a library or archive's ability to make copies of complete works for the purposes of preservation or replacement.

(b) The rights of reproduction and distribution under this section apply to three copies or phonorecords of an unpublished work duplicated solely for purposes of preservation and security or for deposit for research use in another library or archives of the type described by clause (2) of subsection (a), if –

1. the copy or phonorecord reproduced is currently in the collections of the library or archives; and

2. any such copy or phonorecord that is reproduced in digital format is not otherwise distributed in that format and is not made available to the public in that format outside the premises of the library or archives.

(c) The right of reproduction under this section applies to three copies or phonorecords of a published work duplicated solely for the purpose of replacement of a copy or phonorecord that is damaged, deteriorating, lost, or stolen, or if the existing format in which the work is stored has become obsolete, if –

1. the library or archives has, after a reasonable effort, determined that an unused replacement cannot be obtained at a fair price; and

2. any such copy or phonorecord that is reproduced in digital format is not made available to the public in that format outside the premises of the library or archives in lawful possession of such copy.

For purposes of this subsection, a format shall be considered obsolete if the machine or device necessary to render perceptible a work stored in that format is no longer manufactured or is no longer reasonably available in the commercial marketplace.

Because libraries generally do not own the contents in an online licensed resource, and there is rarely a physical manifestation of the work that can deteriorate or be lost or stolen, this paragraph does not apply to most electronic resources. CD-ROMs may be covered, however, if the accompanying license does not prohibit duplication for preservation purposes.

Interlibrary loan

Interlibrary lending of library materials is a cooperative service offered between and among libraries across the country. This function allows libraries to give their researchers access to rare, expensive or unusual materials, and not spend collection dollars in doing so. Section 108(d) permits library copying done for this purpose. The section states:

> (d) The rights of reproduction and distribution under this section apply to a copy, made from the collection of a library or archives where the user makes his or her request or from that of another library or archives, of no more than one article or other contribution to a copyrighted collection or periodical issue, or to a copy or phonorecord of a small part of any other copyrighted work, if –
>
> 1. the copy or phonorecord becomes the property of the user, and the library or archives has had no notice that the copy or phonorecord would be used for any purpose other than private study, scholarship, or research; and
> 2. the library or archives displays prominently, at the place where orders are accepted, and includes on its order form, a warning of copyright in accordance

with requirements that the Register of Copyrights shall prescribe by regulation.

In the print environment, publishers were concerned that they were losing subscriptions because libraries were borrowing articles instead of subscribing to a journal. The copyright law addresses this concern in section 108(g)(2), which states that the borrowing library should not request materials in such large quantities from certain publications 'to substitute for a subscription to or purchase of such work'. Like most sections, this clause does not specify how many requests would be considered excessive, so libraries and publishers agreed upon a series of guidelines to do this. The National Commission on New Technological Uses of Copyrighted Works (CONTU) established specific protocols to address these publisher concerns. It is important to note that the CONTU protocols, the previously mentioned CONFU protocols and any other set of guidelines do not have the force of law behind them. They are agreed-upon parameters among interested parties, but they are not legally binding. The full CONTU report is available at the Coalition for Networked Information website (www.cni.org/docs/infopols/CONTU.html).

In the electronic environment, the landscape has changed. Libraries can take advantage of the rights permitted under section 108 if the resource is purchased outright. But since we license access to our electronic resources, we are not automatically permitted to copy these materials to fulfill interlibrary loan requests or to preserve the content. This becomes problematic for those libraries that have cancelled their print journal subscriptions in favor of the electronic version, yet still need to use the same content to provide traditional library services. The good news is that more and more licenses permit the uses articulated in section 108, if appropriate, although exactly how that service is provided may be specified. In the case of interlibrary loan, the lending institution is generally required to print out a copy of the article and use a secure transmission system, such as Ariel, to send the article to the borrowing institution. Publishers prefer this transmission method over sending a digital copy directly to the borrower, because Ariel degrades the quality of the image, indicating that the item being sent is a copy and not the original. Ariel also automatically deletes the electronic version of the article once the borrowing institution receives the faxed copy.

Educational performance exemption

The other sections of Title 17 not discussed here detail further uses third parties are permitted to make of copyrighted works. Section 110, however, is different because it focuses primarily on audiovisual works, which are beyond the scope of the other exemptions. Although video materials are usually not included in the electronic information products that are the focus of this book, video and DVD distributors are now choosing to license their media content rather than selling it outright. The person responsible for managing licensing needs to be aware of the uses the library's constituents are allowed to make of these works under section 110, in addition to those rights granted under copyright, and not agree to a license that takes these rights away.

The real issue with video is displaying or performing the work. Normally, showing a DVD to an audience would require the person or group sponsoring the screening to obtain permission from the copyright holder. This is done either through a one-time license, which is how feature films are managed, or through the purchase of public performance rights. Public performance rights, if available, may be purchased at the time the library acquires the video, and can add hundreds of dollars to the cost. But if the only use your institution will make of a video is for screening in the classroom or for personal check-out, then public performance rights are unnecessary. Section 110 states that it is not a violation of copyright law to use a video or DVD in the following manner:

> (1) performance or display of a work by instructors or pupils in the course of face-to-face teaching activities of a nonprofit educational institution, in a classroom or similar place devoted to instruction, unless, in the case of a motion picture or other audiovisual work, the performance, or the display of individual images, is given by means of a copy that was not lawfully made under this title, and that the person responsible for the performance knew or had reason to believe was not lawfully made.

This means that the screening of any kind of video or DVD in the classroom as part of a course is permitted without the need to pay any additional licensing fees. But the video or DVD screened must be legitimate; it cannot be an illegal copy. If the institution that acquires a video intends to use it for any kind of programming outside of scheduled courses, then public performance rights or permission from the copyright holder are required. This is true even if admission fees are not charged. Many licenses that arrive with videos or DVDs attempt to take the classroom performance rights granted through section 110 away, by requiring additional payments or permissions to use the title in this manner. Such terms and conditions should not be agreed to.

Copyright versus contract law

All of the exemptions outlined above are granted to the person or institutional representative making use of a copyrighted work. These permissions are quite broad and flexible, rather than proscriptive. The intention in writing Title 17 was to encourage the author, artist and inventor to continue their work, while also encouraging and assisting those teaching and conducting research, because both groups' works benefit society as a whole. This flexibility disappears when an institution signs a license or contract. If language in the license specifically prohibits certain behaviors, even if they are permitted under copyright law, you may not use the work in that manner.

In order to preserve these rights, the license negotiator has some options. One is to add a clause to the license that includes language similar to:

> Nothing in this License shall in any way exclude, modify or affect any of the Licensee's or Authorized User's statutory rights under Title 17 of the United States Code (US copyright law).

This language reinstates those rights granted under US copyright law, in case any were prohibited specifically in the license. Some licenses may then specifically include clauses permitting interlibrary loan and electronic reserves, if they want to specify the format of the information being used for these purposes.

Rarely, however, will an information provider agree to the inclusion of such a broad-based clause. Rather, it will want to negotiate each use individually. The negotiator will need to determine which uses are important to his/her institution, and ensure that appropriate language is included. Some licenses may contain a clause that specifically restores those uses authorized through fair use. For example:

> Nothing in this Agreement is intended to limit in any way whatsoever the Licensee's or any Authorized User's rights under the Fair Use provisions of the US copyright law to use the Licensed Materials.

More commonly found is language that permits those activities libraries commonly perform or facilitate, such as interlibrary loan and electronic reserves. Some sample language may be:

> The Subscriber may supply to an Authorized User of another library (whether by post or fax or secure transmission, using Ariel or its equivalent, whereby the electronic file is deleted immediately after printing), for the purposes of research or private study and not for commercial use, a single paper copy of an electronic original of an individual document being part of the Licensed Materials.
>
> The Licensee agrees to fulfill such requests in compliance with section 108 of the US copyright law (17 USC 108, 'Limitations on exclusive rights; Reproduction by libraries and archives') and the Guidelines for the Proviso of Subsection 108(g)(2) prepared by the National Commission on New Technological Uses of Copyrighted Works (CONTU).

This language permits the use of a printed copy of an article, not direct electronic transmission. The following clause permits electronic reserves:

> The Subscriber may incorporate individual articles, chapters or items of the Licensed Materials in electronic

reserve collections for the use of Authorized Users in the course of instruction at the Subscriber's institution, but not for commercial use. Each such item shall carry appropriate acknowledgement of the source, listing title and author of the extract, title and author of the work, and the publisher.

A similar statement may also permit using the resource for print course packs. Requesting these uses may be inappropriate for some products, and therefore the publisher may not accept some or all of these clauses. For example, requesting permission to use an indexing and abstracting service for either interlibrary loan or electronic reserves does not make sense. But if the product contains any full-text journal articles, and the subscribing institution sees the need to use this content for either of these purposes, then language permitting it should be added.

License negotiators need to understand what rights are automatically granted to them and their institutions when they use a copyrighted work under US law. This knowledge can then be applied to contract negotiation. Including most or all of these rights will make internal management of the product easier for you and the rest of your library's staff. Although we know that our staff and users are not for the most part proficient in US copyright law, they are more aware of the rights granted under the law than they are of licensing terms and conditions. The more closely you can make those licensing terms reflect copyright, the easier it will be to convey permitted uses to your faculty, students and library staff.

Note

1. The complete text of Title 17 is available from the US Copyright Office website (www.copyright.gov/title17/). All quotations from Title 17 in this text were retrieved from this website.

2

Who are you? Identifying your institution and its needs

Before licensing an electronic resource, you need to understand your institution, your different user populations and the kinds of uses your library's various constituencies may need or want to make of the product. And, based on local or institutional mandates, or even state law, certain terms and conditions will have to be included in, or excluded from, the license. You also will need to understand the basics behind your institution's computing infrastructure, because most contracts include technical requirements with which your university must comply. The best way to understand your library and institutional structure and needs is to conduct an institutional inventory, resulting in a template which you can use when reviewing all electronic resource contracts. Each product will have a different contract and will serve different institutional and user needs, so your template will be useful, as it will offer guidance in conducting the majority of your negotiations. A sample institutional checklist can be found in Appendix III.

Institutional characteristics

Understanding the type of institution for which you are licensing is the first step in the negotiation process. The contractual obligations of state institutions can be very different from those for a private college or university. State institutions are often defined as state agencies, and therefore must conform to all laws and standard contracting policies established by the state government. Learning what these laws and policies are can be difficult. Large state universities will probably have an office responsible for purchasing goods and services for all units. This department may be called 'purchasing services', 'procurement services' or 'business services'. People in this department will be aware of state licensing requirements, and will be useful resources as you begin to learn about state rules. The contract sections for which your state will have established guidelines will probably be those terms and conditions that discuss the institution's legal responsibilities. These state contract guidelines will not focus on the sections that articulate how you and your community can use the product. The following concepts will be addressed in more detail in the chapters about licensing terms and conditions, but, briefly, the sections of concern to the state may include the following.

- *Indemnity clauses.* These are the clauses that discuss who will be responsible, both legally and financially, if a third party sues the subscriber, the information provider, or both. State agencies are usually prohibited from indemnifying a third party, or someone who is not a participant in the agreement.
- *Liability clauses.* Liability clauses in information resource contracts often state that the information provider waives all financial responsibility for certain events, or, if it does not waive fiscal responsibility, it limits the amount of damages it will pay to the annual subscription fee for the product. Some state agencies are not permitted to agree to a limitation of liability.

- *Jurisdiction and arbitration.* These two sections, if included in a contract, usually appear in close proximity to each other. The jurisdiction is the state whose law governs how the contract will be interpreted, and the location in which any conflicts concerning the agreement will be heard. State agencies may be prohibited from agreeing to any jurisdiction outside their home state. They may also be prohibited from agreeing to binding arbitration, because the location of the arbitration agency may be outside the state, or may not be indicated.

State agencies may be required to agree to or remove other terms and conditions in a contract. If your institution's purchasing office is not able to help, your state procurement office should be able to provide you with state-mandated contract language that will give you the information you need. If neither of these offices can help, contact your institution's legal office. Electronic resource librarians working on behalf of private colleges and universities do not have the force of state law to support their negotiations. Instead, institutional policy will govern what terms and conditions are acceptable, and which must be rejected. Those mentioned above – indemnity, liability and jurisdiction – should be negotiated to protect your institution. Strategies for requesting contract language changes will be discussed in the contract terms and conditions section of this text.

Another institutional characteristic that must be considered is the geographic structure. Because 'authorized site' definitions, specifying physical locations where product access will be permitted, are included in some electronic resource licenses, you need to be aware of the physical and administrative structure of your college or university. The primary issue for some institutions will be whether the licensed product's access will be permitted for more than one geographic site. A second site may be as small as a research office ten miles from campus, or as large as a second location in a state-wide university system. Depending upon the license, multiple physical locations may change the nature of the license agreement and the cost of the product.

User populations

Equally as important as knowing your physical institutional structure is defining your user populations. Most contracts will have a section entitled 'authorized users' or something similar that will define who has permission to use the product. One piece of information you should have available at all times is your college or university's full-time equivalent count, or FTE. This figure is your enrollment, which combines part-time students in order to come up with the number of students who, in total, would be attending full time. This figure is usually based upon the fall semester enrollment figures, and officially established at some time in the middle of that semester, after enrollment has been certified. The other count you may need, although information providers do not request it as often, is a head count. That number counts each student as one enrollee, whether they are full or part time. Your registrar's office will be able to provide you with both figures. If you are affiliated with a large research institution, a more granular FTE count may be necessary. Enrollment numbers can be broken down by status: graduate students, undergraduate students and professional school student enrollments. These figures may prove useful, depending on the product being negotiated and the appropriate audience for that product.

You may find that you need your FTE count broken down even further, into enrollment by individual college or major.

These figures are more difficult to isolate, but your registrar or the college or subject department office should be able to provide its own enrollment figure. Rarely will an information provider request enrollments by college, but if you are negotiating access to a highly specialized product, basing the price on the number of likely users rather than the institution's overall enrollment may be a way to reduce the product's subscription cost.

Where your users live and work will also influence contract negotiations. Do the vast majority of students reside on campus, or do most or all live off campus and commute? Will your faculty want access from their homes as well as from their offices? If you want your users to have the ability to access electronic resources from off campus, you must include remote-access language in the contract. You will also need to have the technical infrastructure in place to restrict access to only those authorized users affiliated with your institution.

Finally, your user population may include members of your local community. If you must or want to provide public access to your electronic resources, then your contract will need to permit this explicitly. Known as walk-in users, members of the general public will be permitted to access the resource from within your library, but will not, as a rule, be able to access the content from their homes or any other locations off campus.

Library uses

Negotiations are not only with the company providing access to the resource you are licensing, but are also with parties within your library. Those who manage interlibrary loan and electronic reserves departments, and even the head of preservation, have a vested interest in how they are able to use the electronic products you license – particularly if the library's collection managers have decided to cancel print journal subscriptions in favor of the electronic counterparts. Continuing to have the ability to use electronic journals and full-text aggregator products as they would print journals will be of particular importance. To determine your colleagues' needs, you should meet with all interested parties and discuss their requirements as they relate to the content in your institution's licensed resources.

Network and security infrastructure

Once you know the geographic structure of your institution, your user populations and your library's needs, you must then understand the computing network that will manage content access for your users, and prevent access by those who are not affiliated with your college or university. Understanding your technical infrastructure includes knowing your institution's internet protocol, or IP, addresses. You will need to know whether a proxy server is used to regulate access to the campus network from outside the institution. Knowing these and other details about your computer system is important, because most contracts you read will require your institution to meet certain technical and security specifications. The following is not intended to be an exhaustive look at a university's computing and network services; rather, it should serve as a brief introduction. You will need to work with your library and university computing offices to make sure you have enough understanding of your local services and systems to allow you to negotiate agreements for products whose access and security will rely on your institution's computing infrastructure.

Secure network

Simply put, a secure network is one whose access is restricted to authorized users only. Almost all licenses will require the subscribing institution to have a secure network, so those not affiliated with the institution cannot gain access to the product's contents. As the negotiator of the agreement, you need to be certain that your institution can comply with this requirement.

IP addresses

An IP address is a unique identifying number assigned to a specific port on a computer network. It is used by electronic devices, such as computers, to identify the computer with which they are interacting. Blocks of IP addresses are assigned to internet service providers. Most colleges and universities are considered internet service providers, because they manage their population's access to the internet through their own networks. You will need to know your institution's IP addresses, because the information provider will use them as one way to identify that a user is trying to access its resource from a computer on your campus. Most colleges and universities will have a couple of either Class B or Class C ranges, or a portion of either type. A range consists of a series of numbers, and may also contain a star, or wild card, meaning that all numbers following the initial number are part of that range. For example, the following are some of the ranges registered at this time to the Pennsylvania State University:

Class B range	128.118.*.*
Class C range	64.74.144.*
Portion of a Class C range	66.71.1–127.*

IP addresses are public information – anyone can identify the owner of a specific IP address, or can find a list of IP addresses assigned to an institution or internet provider through a simple web search. Just as someone mailing a letter knows that it will be delivered to the address they place on the envelope, a computer sending information to one of the IP addresses shown above knows that the information will be delivered to a computer residing on Penn State University's network.

Proxy server

A proxy server is essentially a gatekeeper, preventing unauthorized users from accessing resources on a secure network and permitting those who are authorized, after identifying themselves, to gain access. More technically, it is a server assigned an IP address on the college or university's network. Authorized users who are not using a computer on campus, and who are attempting to gain access to an electronic resource protected by a secure network, will be directed first to the proxy server. The proxy server will request that the user identifies herself, usually by means of an ID/password. Once the user's identity is confirmed, the proxy server will permit access to the resource. The information provider's computer will not see the address where the authorized user is sitting, because that address is not within the subscribing institution's address list. Rather, it will see the address of the proxy server, and thus identify the user as someone requesting access from a subscribing institution. Some license agreements will ask if your institution is using a proxy server, and require you to identify the IP address assigned. They request this information because the proxy server will probably register many more users than other addresses within the institution's IP ranges.

ID/password management

Most information providers manage subscriber access to their resources based on institutional IP addresses. A few smaller publishers, however, continue to regulate access to their products through ID/passwords they supply to the subscribing institution. Designed for the individual subscriber, ID/password-controlled access is cumbersome for an institution to manage. The most efficient way to provide access to such a product is through the creation of a script, which is a program that automatically enters the ID/password into the publisher's site. To guarantee access security, such a program might funnel users through the proxy server first, requiring them to log into the campus network prior to accessing the resource. You should consult with your technical support department to determine if scripting is a viable option for your library. If your programmers cannot script the ID/password, or the information provider will not permit you to do so (you *must* ask permission to do this!), you will need to find an alternative method to manage access to the product, or not license the resource at all.

Responding to security and license breaches

Despite the network security you have in place, and the information concerning appropriate use of licensed resources you have provided, inevitably someone will violate your contract. An unauthorized user might gain access to your network, but more likely the breach will be caused by an authorized user. They might set up a robot, which is a program designed to search for and download all content corresponding to established search terms. Or they might systematically download the entire contents of whole journal titles, or even entire databases. Both activities are almost always specifically prohibited. The use of a robot can slow down the responsiveness of a product's server for all subscribers. Information providers are more concerned about systematic downloading of whole journals and databases, obviously, because the perpetrator is stealing their content.

When a security or license breach occurs, the information provider will probably be the first to detect an unusually large amount of activity, since it is able to monitor database traffic on its servers. If the breach is serious, such as systematic downloading, the company will probably shut down the IP address where this activity is occurring, and then notify you. To be in compliance with most of your license agreements, you will need to have a process in place to address this activity. Such a process will include working with the information provider and your network personnel to identify the user, notifying the user that his/her behavior violates your contract with the publisher and requesting restoration of access to the product. Table 2.1 shows one possible breach management process.

A part of this process is notifying the abuser, who should be identifiable through the IP address used and any authentication information the user had to enter prior to accessing the database. Contacting the suspected abuser through e-mail is efficient, and is a necessity if product access has been suspended. A cease-and-desist letter informs them of their violation and the possible consequences to them personally and to the institution as a whole. Such a letter could resemble the following:

Dear Student

Acme Information Company has notified the University Library that you were detected systematically downloading all issues of the journals available from

Table 2.1	Database breach management process

All notifications of a breach should be sent to the electronic resources librarian (ERL), with copies to the assistant dean for collections and the head of Library Computing.

1. ERL contacts the electronic resources provider and requests:

   a. exact information concerning the breach (time, IP, information downloaded);
   b. restoration of database access.

2. After breach information is received from the vendor, ERL forwards it to head of Library Computing.

3. Library Computing identifies user and forwards information to ERL.

4. ERL contacts user, outlines his/her reported behavior, and explains licensing terms and consequences for continued misuse of the product.

5. ERL forwards the same message to vendor contact, deleting user name and ID*, so vendor is aware that the issue has been addressed as required in the product's license agreement.

6. ERL notifies appropriate subject selector of breach, without revealing the user's identity.

7. If the user commits a second violation, the case is then referred to the director of Network Security for further action.

* You must not share the name of the user with the company representative, as this is a violation of privacy laws, including the Family Educational Rights and Privacy Act (FERPA).

the American Society of Basketry and Knitting. Our licensing agreement with Acme Information Company, which allows us to provide access to its product to the entire university community, strictly prohibits this behavior. Your activity has resulted in the university losing access to these journals, and jeopardizes our ability to work with Acme in the future to restore access.

You must cease the systematic downloading of content immediately, and delete the content that you have already downloaded. Continued misuse of licensed electronic resources could result in your loss of computing privileges. I would be happy to explain why this activity is inappropriate, and to help you understand the potential ramifications of such behavior for the university.

Thank you for your immediate action concerning this matter. Please contact me if you have any questions.

Sincerely,

Electronic Resources Librarian

While the language may seem severe, your users need to understand that their behavior is not only inappropriate, but could result in permanent loss of access to the product. Surprisingly, most people who systematically download content or use a robot to data mine do not have any idea that their actions are a violation of your agreement.

Conclusion

Becoming aware of your institution is the very first step you should take before attempting to negotiate an agreement for an electronic resource. Every college and university is different. Each serves a unique population with differing needs, and these needs will change depending upon the type of resource you are licensing. Administrative and collection management decisions internal to the library will also shape the licensing process. You and your colleagues should discuss internal needs and goals, along with the needs of the user community, before beginning the negotiation process. And, finally, every institution's computer systems are different. They are structured and managed differently. Spending time with the relevant computer services people, both internal and external to the library, in order to learn about security and access management will prove very useful. You will understand what kind of network security your institution can provide, and your computing people will become partners in managing access to these products.

3

The license

Introduction

You now know what you and your users are permitted to do with a copyrighted work under US copyright law, and you have a clear understanding of your institution, users and computing infrastructure. Now it is time to learn about the document that defines whether you can continue to exercise your copyrights, if your users will be permitted to access and use the information within a product to their satisfaction, or even if your institution will be able to subscribe to the product at all. This document is the license. The license dictates what is in the product, how it can be used, how it may not be used and who is responsible for how it is used. When you or your institution's authorized signatory sign a license, you are obligating your college or university administration and community to behave within the parameters outlined in the terms and conditions of the document. As the first, and perhaps the last, person to read the license, you need to understand that this document legally binds your institution to the terms and conditions contained therein. Therefore, you must know what the language in the license means, and how it impacts your users, library and institution.

This chapter will not only provide definitions of common terms found in an electronic resources license, but will also go through a sample license section by section, discussing the purpose of each and offering guidance on which areas may raise concerns. This exercise will act as an introduction to a long and complex legal document. As you begin to read other licenses, you will notice they use similar, or even identical, terms and conditions, because information providers tend to be concerned about the same issues. Recognizing the similarities in these licenses will expedite the review process. You will know where problems may lie, and what language needs to be removed and what needs to be added to make the contract acceptable to your users and institution.

Defining two important terms offers a logical introduction to this chapter. These terms are *license* and *contract*. We discuss licensing terms and conditions, but we are in fact negotiating a contract and thus contract law governs our behavior. Although we use the terms license and contract interchangeably, and I will do so in this book, their definitions are slightly different.

License

So, what is a license? The term might bring a document like a driver's license to mind. A driver's license is a physical object certifying that the holder has passed an exam and has been granted the privilege of driving. In more general terms a license is 'the permission granted by competent authority to exercise a certain privilege that, without such authorization, would constitute an illegal act' (Phelps and Lehman, 2004, Vol. 6: 313). So a license is a legal permission to use or do something. In the case of an electronic resource, the information provider owns the rights to the content of a product, or has the right to offer access to that resource, usually in exchange for a fee. Thus it is able to license that resource to us, or give us permission to use it. The document that establishes the terms and conditions under which the information provider is willing to grant us permission to use the resource, however, is the contract.

Contract

A contract is an agreement between parties 'creating an enforceable obligation to do, or to refrain from doing, a particular thing' (ibid., Vol. 3: 167). In order for a contract to exist, both parties must agree to the terms and conditions expressed within the document, and the signers of the contract must have the authority within their organizations to commit to the obligations spelled out in the document. For libraries, most of the contracts we manage are *express contracts*, in which the terms and conditions are explicitly offered by one party – most frequently in writing – and accepted by another. We do, however, encounter a variety of other types of contracts that do not require a signature in order to bind the institution to the terms and conditions. These may be known as end-user, shrink-wrap, click-through or click-wrap licenses. Collectively, these contracts are called *adhesion contracts*, because one party holds all the rights and the other party must agree to the terms presented without the opportunity to negotiate. The subscriber need only perform a designated action, such as clicking an 'I agree' button, in order to be bound by the responsibilities spelled out in the contract. The simple act of using a product can also create a valid agreement between the parties, if so indicated in an accompanying contract. A user may also become bound by an adhesion contract by *not* doing something. For example, if the user does not return a product within 30 days of receipt, she may then be bound by the terms of an accompanying agreement. These types of contracts are easier for the licensing entity to manage. Very little or no paperwork is involved. And, because such a contract does not encourage negotiations, the same terms and conditions bind every user. Needless to say, these contracts are not consumer-friendly – people are not inclined to read the terms of a click-through agreement, so most consumers have no idea what they are agreeing to. But if a person has a physical, paper contract in front of her, she is more inclined to read the agreement prior to signing. For some libraries, particularly state institutions, accepting adhesion contracts is not permitted – contracts binding a state entity require an authorized signature. I would strongly encourage those negotiators who work for institutions that permit their departments to agree to adhesion contracts to get a signed agreement as well. Having that document in your file or those data in your electronic resource management system will make the product easier to manage. Because my institution requires a signed version of a click-through agreement, I notify the information provider, so we can work out any necessary logistics. I amend the document, or at the very least add signatory lines resembling those in the license in Appendix I, print out the document and mail it to the information provider.

The differences between a license and a contract are few. In our case, the license is giving us permission to access and use a resource. The contract documents this permission and outlines the specific terms and conditions that inform our use of the product. The next section will analyze the terms and conditions found in a standard electronic resource contract.

Parts of the contract

Although most electronic resource contracts contain unique language, they tend to have similar components. Sections containing the same information may be labeled or organized differently from one contract to the next. The labels are there to organize the terms and conditions contained in the document, and to help both licensor and subscriber identify specific portions of the contract as they negotiate the language within each section.

In order to have a common document with which to discuss both how a contract is organized and how the terms and conditions within the contract are defined, I obtained permission from a scholarly society to use its contract as a sample. The basis of this document is a model license John Cox and Associates, the authoring agency, has placed in the public domain. The scholarly society made some modifications to the public document, and I have made a small number of changes as well. At the society's request, I have removed its identity from the document. The full sample license is shown in Appendix I.

For our purposes, the Acme Information Company is the licensing entity, managing the content of the American Society of Basketry and Knitting. The content licensed under the original contract consisted of the society's publications: electronic journals, books and proceedings. Since the components of a contract are similar whether the licensed product is an electronic journal or an indexing and abstracting service, the following discussion about terms and conditions in our sample license can be applied broadly.

Parties to the contract

The first portion of most licensing agreements specifies the parties involved in the contract. The name of each party (the company with the rights to the product, and the library or institution licensing the product) will be indicated, along with contact information such as a mailing address. In our sample license, the parties to the contract are the Acme Information Company and Large State University. This section might also contain the date upon which the contract becomes valid, which in this case is 1 January 2008. For management purposes you might alter this date to coincide with the date you want access to begin – at the beginning of the month, the calendar year or the fiscal year – and not necessarily the date when the agreement is received or signed.

Key definitions

If a section defining important terms is present in the agreement, it usually follows immediately after the parties to the contract are identified. A key definitions section ensures that both parties have a common language when referring to terms that either party could misinterpret. You, as the person negotiating on behalf of your library, should read these definitions carefully. If they do not reflect your understanding of those terms as they are commonly used in your institution, you should amend them accordingly. The following terms are defined in our sample license – an electronic resource contract may include other definitions, or may use different terms to describe similar services or concepts.

Authorized users

This definition specifies who is permitted access to the information resource. They may include students, faculty and staff. These users may be permitted to access the resource from within the library, from other locations on campus and from off campus as well. Registered users or members of the community who are in the library may also be permitted to use the product. The sample license offers a thorough, inclusive definition of authorized users:

> Current members of the faculty and other staff of the Subscriber (whether on a permanent, temporary, contract or visiting basis) and individuals who are currently studying at the Subscriber's institution, who are permitted to access the Secure Network from within the Library Premises or from such other places where Authorized Users work or study (including but not limited to Authorized Users' offices and homes, halls of residence and student dormitories) and who have been issued by the Subscriber with a password or other authentication, together with other persons who are permitted to use the Subscriber's library or information service and access the Secure Network but only from computer terminals within the Library Premises.

Notice that your students, faculty and staff are granted specific permission to access the resource remotely. Those members of the local community who are not permitted to log into the college or university's network, otherwise known as walk-in users, may still use the product, but they must access it in the library.

Authorized site

While our sample contract does not contain this term in the key definitions section, many contracts define a geographic location within which a licensed resource may be used. The most restrictive site definitions limit an authorized site to a specific geographic radius from the subscribing library (often five miles). Others define the site as a single geographic campus, which may or may not include any satellite locations within the same city limits. Still other site definitions may include distant campuses if those locations are managed or administered by the primary campus.

Commercial use

This definition means any use of the resource, either by a representative of the licensing institution or by an authorized user, for monetary gain.

Course packs

This term refers to print booklets of assigned readings compiled for a specific class, which may be used in place of a course textbook. If a license permits the use of a product for course pack preparation, the department on campus responsible for compiling these readings is not required to pay royalties if it operates on a cost-recovery basis. Commercial printing companies that prepare course packs for the same institution, however, would be required to pay royalties for the same articles, and would pass along those costs to students, because the production and distribution of this aggregated content is done for commercial purposes.

Electronic reserves

While electronic reserves serve a similar function as a course pack, this service does not distribute print copies of course readings. Rather, the library creates an electronic file of requested readings, either through links to a licensed resource or by scanning a print text. These readings are provided in digital format only, and their access is restricted to students registered for a specific course.

Fee

This is the amount the subscriber is expected to pay for access to the resource.

Library premises

This definition may be the same as the 'authorized site' definition presented above, or it may refer specifically to the building or buildings housing the library.

Licensed materials

This refers to the content being licensed. The definition may refer the person reading the document to an appendix detailing the products or services the subscriber is licensing. Our sample contract delineates the licensed materials in Schedule 1.

Secure network

This is a stand-alone or virtual network within the internet, accessible to authorized users only, who are identified by the subscribing institution at the time of the user's log-in or through an internet protocol (IP) address. Security measures are expected to conform to current best practices.

Server

In this license, the server refers to the information provider's hardware where the licensed contents are housed and maintained.

Subscription period

This is the period of time for which access to the electronic content will be provided, as designated in this contract.

Agreement

The publisher or information provider will usually outline, in very broad terms, what services it is offering, and the terms under which it is offering this service. Within this section, the contract will probably state that the agreement is *non-exclusive* (the publisher can offer this service to more than one entity) and *non-transferable* (the subscriber cannot offer the service to a third party). This section also contains language stating that the subscriber does not obtain copyright to the licensed content through this contract. Either the publisher or the original copyright owner retains exclusive rights granted to them under the law, as discussed in Chapter 1.

Other concepts covered in this section include the term of the agreement and post-cancellation access. In our sample license, the *term* of the agreement is one year. The agreement will automatically terminate at the end of the year, unless both the subscriber and the information provider agree to renew it. A section labeled 'term and termination' appears later in the license, which specifies the conditions under which this agreement can be terminated prior to the end of the contract year. *Post-cancellation access* language may appear under a section outlining an information provider's responsibilities, or it might be found in the section that articulates the publisher's policy concerning archival access. What is the difference between post-cancellation and archival access? Post-cancellation access means providing access to those issues of a journal to which a library subscribed that were published during the length of the agreement. Even if the agreement ends, the library's users would continue to have access to those journal issues – just as they would if the library had purchased the issues in print. Acme Information Company does not ensure that post-cancellation access to this content will be provided through its current interface. It offers the content in a portable format, such as a CD-ROM, or through a third party with which it will contract to provide both post-cancellation and archival access. Archival access is offered to those libraries that maintain a current subscription to the content. In this license, a discussion of archival access occurs later in the contract.

Usage rights

This section, which also might be labeled 'terms of use' or 'use of product', specifies what authorized users, the licensing institution, or both may do with the content of the information resource. The sample license we are using distinguishes between the rights assigned to the subscribing institution and those granted to an individual user, although many contracts do not separate the two entities. The institution's usage rights are delineated first. A library staff member, as a representative of the institution, is permitted to:

> 3.1.1 Make such local electronic copies by means of caching or mirrored storage of all or part of the Licensed Materials as are necessary solely to ensure efficient use by Authorized Users.

This clause may seem unnecessary, because caching is a standard computer function. The contents are copied on the computer's hard drive to expedite access. Some contracts explicitly permit this activity, and others do not mention it. Although few information providers would consider copying via caching a violation of the contract, you might consider adding such language to protect your library.

The library may also:

> 3.1.2 Allow Authorized Users to have access to the Licensed Materials from the Server via the Secure Network.

The library is authorized, in this clause, to provide access to the product's content through a network that limits access to authorized users only. Many licenses do not include this language, as this is how libraries tend to provide and manage secure access.

A library may:

> 3.1.3 Provide Authorized Users with integrated access and an integrated author, article title, abstract and keyword index to the Licensed Materials and all other similar material licensed from other publishers.

Basically, this clause permits the subscribing library to use another interface to access this content. One example would be using an open URL link resolver to search an index, then linking to the full-text content offered through this product.

The library is permitted to:

> 3.1.4 Provide single printed or electronic copies of single articles or chapters of the Licensed Materials at the request of individual Authorized Users.

With the proliferation of printers, few libraries continue to offer copying services to their users. If such a service is still available, however, this clause permits the subscribing library to create a single hard copy of an article for an authorized user, reminiscent of the right a library or archive has through section 108 of the copyright law.

A library staff member may:

> 3.1.5 Display, download or print the Licensed Materials for the purpose of internal marketing or testing or for training Authorized Users or groups of Authorized Users.

This clause permits making hard copies, digital copies or projecting of the product's contents for internal training or library instruction.

The above language may seem superfluous, as those of us who work in libraries assume that using any electronic resource to perform these activities is permitted. While very few information providers would prohibit a library employee from engaging in most, if not all, of these activities, Acme Information Company is being thorough, eliminating potential confusion and reducing the number of requested contract changes by including this language in the agreement. Some licenses may articulate other permitted institutional uses in this section, such as interlibrary loan, course pack use and electronic reserves. Our sample license addresses these uses later in the document.

The next section outlines those uses an individual authorized user may make of the content of this product. Like the institutional rights articulated above, these rights seem obvious, but are included to reduce ambiguity. They include the following.

- 3.2.1 *Search, view, retrieve and display the Licensed Materials.* A critical right your students, faculty and staff members need to make use of this product.

- 3.2.2 *Electronically save individual articles, chapters or items of the Licensed Materials for personal use.* Users will tend to save content, with or without permission, so it is best to have this permission articulated. The larger question, as it was when discussing fair use, is how much. By stating that a user is permitted to save an individual article or chapter, this contract implies that saving an entire book or journal issue would not be permitted. This language also reinforces that the content must be saved for personal, not commercial, use.

- 3.2.3 *Print off a copy of individual articles, chapters or items of the Licensed Materials.* All users print content, so again the amount permitted, both explicitly and implicitly, is of more interest than the activity itself.

- 3.2.4 *Distribute a copy of individual articles, chapters or items of the Licensed Materials in print or electronic form to other Authorized Users.* This permitted use not only allows an individual to send a portion of the product's content to another authorized user, it also allows a faculty member to put content from this product into the institution's course management system, as long as access is restricted to authorized users only. Faculty members may also distribute print copies to students in their classes, as is permitted under the fair use provision of copyright.

Other permitted uses may be found in this section of an electronic resource license, although they are not part of our sample license. If they are not, you may want to include the following.

- *Reproduce an insubstantial portion of an article from the resource for educational, non-commercial use.* This language reinforces the user's right to cite this work in another work, as permitted under fair use.

- *Authorized users are permitted to share insubstantial portions of the licensed material with an unauthorized user for the purposes of research and scholarship only.* The permission granted under this clause is called scholarly sharing. Users are permitted to share copies of individual articles or a small portion of the product with others affiliated with non-subscribing institutions for non-profit research and education purposes only. This clause may mandate that the material cannot be shared in electronic form – the article or chapter in question must be printed and mailed.

This section can become a laundry list of uses you want available to your students, faculty and staff. One way to prevent this from occurring, as discussed in Chapter 1, is to insert a clause into the contract that retains all of your users' and institutional rights under copyright law. The following clause might be used: 'Nothing in this License shall in any way exclude, modify or affect any of the Subscriber's or Authorized Users' statutory rights under US copyright law.' Our sample contract has a similar clause, but it does not include the words 'authorized users', meaning that the library is permitted to make use of the product as outlined in section 108, which are those rights reserved for libraries and archives. All rights granted under the law to individuals, however, particularly under fair use, are not expressly permitted under our sample contract's 'usage rights' section.

Interlibrary loan

While section 3.3, permitting uses already allowed under section 108 of US copyright law, makes some of the language in this section duplicative, 4.1 has been included in our sample license because it specifies the physical format to be used when fulfilling a request. In most licensing agreements where interlibrary loan is permitted, the lending library is required to print out a copy of the requested article, then send it through Ariel, a fax-like transmission system. Rarely is a library permitted to use the digital version of an article to fulfill a request. This license requires the same format transformation.

Course packs and electronic reserves

Having permission to use content covered under this license for course pack preparation and electronic reserve services is a benefit to the subscriber. If your campus has a course pack preparation service, that unit will not have to pay royalties to include this content in their packs. And the license permits use of this content for reserve services without permission or additional fees.

Prohibited uses

Along with a 'usage rights' section, a contract may have a separate section explicitly detailing the types of uses an authorized user or subscribing institution may *not* make of the licensed content. Other contracts may combine this section with the previous one, under a broad 'uses' heading. In either case, this section is included to highlight those behaviors or uses that the information provider finds particularly troublesome. The prohibitions included in this section supersede permitted uses outlined in section 3 of our sample contract, as indicated by the inclusion of the phrase 'subject to clause 6 below' in the preface to section 3. Neither the subscribing institution nor an individual user is permitted to use the product in the following manner under the sample license.

- 6.1.1 *Remove or alter the authors' names or the Publisher's copyright notices or other means of identification or disclaimers as they appear in the Licensed Materials.* No one should use a copyrighted work and claim it as her own. This prohibition reiterates that if we use this content for interlibrary loan or reserves, for example, we need to ensure that all identifying information is intact.

- 6.1.2 *Systematically make print or electronic copies of multiple extracts of the Licensed Materials for any purpose other than back-up copies permitted under clause 3.1.2.* Publishers are concerned that individual users will download large quantities of journal or database content, and take it with them when they graduate. Understandably, no information provider wants a bootlegged copy of its product freely available. The inclusion of this language reinforces that prohibition.

- 6.1.3 *Mount or distribute any part of the Licensed Materials on any electronic network, including without limitation the Internet and the World Wide Web, other than the Secure Network.* We are being reminded that the publisher's content should be accessible to authorized users only. Mounting any of the content on a network that is not password protected opens up the content to the world, and jeopardizes the publisher's ability to exercise control over its product.

Our sample license also has a section that specifies some uses that might be permitted if written authorization can be obtained.

6.2 The Publisher's explicit written permission must be obtained in order to:

6.2.1 use all or any part of the Licensed Materials for any Commercial Use;

6.2.2 systematically distribute the whole or any part of the Licensed Materials to anyone other than Authorized Users;

6.2.3 publish, distribute or make available the Licensed Materials, works based on the Licensed Materials or works which combine them with any other material, other than as permitted in this License;

6.2.4 alter, abridge, adapt or modify the Licensed Materials, except to the extent necessary to make them perceptible on a computer screen to Authorized Users. For the avoidance of doubt, no alteration of the words or their order is permitted.

Why list these uses separately? In most licenses they would be included with the other prohibited uses. Most likely they have been listed separately because the publisher could envisage reasons why these uses might be permitted, even if that use would require the subscriber to pay an additional fee. For example, an authorized user offering a workshop may want to distribute an article to participants, not all of whom are affiliated with the licensing institution. The publisher would likely permit this, as it would not lose any income. Inclusion of such a section allows some flexibility, and encourages the subscriber to request permission rather than assuming that the publisher will deny such a request.

If you determine that your institution needs to use the product in any way that is prohibited under this section of the contract, you would remove the prohibiting language and add the use to the 'permitted uses' section.

The language used in the contract up to this point has been relatively straightforward. The following sections become more complex, and create the greatest amount of confusion for library license negotiators.

Publisher's undertakings

In this section the publisher presents its contractual obligations to the subscriber. The very first item in this section is one of the more complex concepts in a license – the publisher's warranty.

Warranty

According to *West's Encyclopedia of American Law*, a warranty is 'an assurance, promise, or guaranty by one party that a particular statement of fact is true and may be relied upon by the other party' (Phelps and Lehman, 2004, Vol. 10: 287). We tend to associate warranties with the purchase of goods such as automobiles or appliances. Warranties for these items guarantee that if something goes wrong with the product, the company will take care of the problem within the parameters stated in the contract. Warranties in general fall into two categories: express and implied. *Expressed* warranties are 'specific promises made by the seller and include oral representations, written representations, descriptions of the goods or services, representations in samples and models, and proof of prior quality of the goods or services' (ibid.: 288). These are the warranties with which we are most familiar – those that accompany a new dishwasher, for example. *Implied* warranties are those that do not need to be in the contract in order to be in effect.

Information providers generally include one or two different warranty clauses in their contracts, each of which has a different purpose. The first warranty type is a guarantee to the subscriber that the information provider either owns the content in the product or has the right to distribute the information contained within the product. It is called a *warranty of title*. This is an implied warranty, meaning that appropriate language need not be included in the contract. Whether a warranty of title is stated or not, the information provider must have the right to license the content in its product, and the subscriber has the right to assume this. Explicit warranty of title language would be similar to the following: 'The licensor warrants that it has the right to distribute the content contained within this product.'

Our sample license contains language that implies a warranty of title:

> 7.1 THE PUBLISHER WARRANTS TO THE SUBSCRIBER THAT THE LICENSED MATERIALS USED AS CONTEMPLATED BY THIS LICENSE DO NOT INFRINGE THE COPYRIGHT OR ANY OTHER PROPRIETARY OR INTELLECTUAL PROPERTY RIGHTS OF ANY PERSON.

If the product does not violate anyone's copyrights, the implication is that the licensor has the right to distribute the resource, and thus can guarantee title. The remaining language in this clause refers to indemnification, which will be discussed later in this chapter. Notice that this section is all in capital letters. This is intentional. Some state laws require licenses to place clauses that are not in the consumer's best interest in all capitals, and/or in bold, guaranteeing that this language will stand out from the rest of the text.

The second type of warranty found frequently in an information resource contract mentions both the warranty of merchantability and the warranty of fitness. Both of these are, by definition, implied warranties. The warranty of merchantability states that the product will do what it is supposed to do. The only qualifying factor is that the person selling or licensing the product is qualified in some manner to sell the product. The warranty of fitness is more complex, because it refers to the ability of a seller to select an appropriate product to fulfill a specified purpose. The person selling the product would have to be aware of the purpose for which the product was being purchased, and know that the buyer is relying on his or her expertise in making a product selection. Also, the buyer must, in making a decision, rely on the seller's expertise. An example would be your decision to go to an appliance store and ask a salesperson to help you select a product that will clean your dishes. You have stated your purpose, and told the salesperson that you are relying on his/her help and you intend to take his/her advice. If the salesperson then suggested that you purchase a refrigerator to clean your dishes, the courts would probably agree that an implied warranty of fitness existed, and that the salesperson violated that warranty.

As you can imagine, no information provider would be willing to offer a warranty of either fitness or merchantability. It could not know how every user intends to utilize the content of its products. Because of the rapid turnover among company representatives, the company could not guarantee that its sales personnel would know the best products for certain uses. And rarely would we, as representatives of our subject selectors and teaching faculty, ask a sales representative for a product recommendation. In order to protect themselves from legal action based on either of these implied warranties, information providers must include a *disclaimer of warranties* in their contracts, which means that they do not make any claims about their products' performance or appropriateness. Our sample contract's disclaimer of warranties clause reads:

7.6 EXCEPT AS EXPRESSLY PROVIDED IN THIS LICENSE, THE PUBLISHER MAKES NO REPRESENTATIONS OR WARRANTIES OF ANY KIND, EXPRESS OR IMPLIED, INCLUDING, BUT NOT LIMITED TO, WARRANTIES OF DESIGN,

ACCURACY OF THE INFORMATION CONTAINED IN THE LICENSED MATERIALS, MERCHANTABILITY OR FITNESS OF USE FOR A PARTICULAR PURPOSE. THE LICENSED MATERIALS ARE SUPPLIED 'AS IS'.

Indemnity clause

The second half of section 7.1 in our sample license refers to the publisher's responsibilities if a third party – someone who is not affiliated with either the information provider or the subscriber – sues the library for copyright infringement. Because the publisher has warranted that it has not violated anyone's copyright in offering its product for lease, it is agreeing to indemnify, or protect, the subscriber. While most of us have experience with warranties, indemnities are an unknown, except perhaps for the phrase 'double indemnity'. Double indemnity is an agreement between an insurance company and a customer guaranteeing that, if the insured person dies under certain circumstances outlined in the agreement, the insurance company will pay twice the policy value. Indemnity clauses in electronic resource contracts are not tied to the death of either party, but they do state the terms and conditions under which one of the licensing parties will pay restitution to the other. The trigger for invoking an indemnity clause's protection may be, as mentioned earlier, a lawsuit brought by a third party.

The following is the rest of section 7.1 of our license:

THE PUBLISHER SHALL INDEMNIFY AND HOLD THE SUBSCRIBER HARMLESS FROM AND AGAINST ANY LOSS, DAMAGE, COSTS, LIABILITY AND EXPENSES (INCLUDING REASONABLE LEGAL AND PROFESSIONAL FEES) ARISING OUT

OF ANY LEGAL ACTION TAKEN AGAINST THE SUBSCRIBER CLAIMING ACTUAL OR ALLEGED INFRINGEMENT OF SUCH RIGHTS. THIS INDEMNITY SHALL SURVIVE THE TERMINATION OF THIS LICENSE FOR ANY REASON. THIS INDEMNITY SHALL NOT APPLY IF THE SUBSCRIBER HAS AMENDED THE LICENSED MATERIALS IN ANY WAY NOT PERMITTED BY THIS LICENSE.

This clause states that, if the subscriber is sued by a third party who claims that the subscriber's use of the content in this product is a violation of its copyrights, the information provider will pay for the subscriber's legal fees and damages. It also states that this indemnity protection will remain in effect even if the agreement is no longer in place, because this publisher is permitting post-cancellation access. One caveat: if the subscriber has done anything with the content not permitted under this contract, and is then sued, the publisher is no longer responsible for any legal fees or penalties.

This is not the only indemnity clause in the contract. Another clause appears under 'subscriber's undertakings', and will be discussed later in this chapter.

Product performance

Other publisher responsibilities specified in this section focus on the availability and accessibility of the content, otherwise know as product performance. The following clauses are those related to how and when content will be available.

Firstly, the publisher must:

7.2.1 Make the Licensed Materials available to the Subscriber from the Server in the media, format and time schedule specified in Schedule 1. The Publisher will notify the Subscriber at least sixty (60) days in advance of any anticipated specification change applicable to the Licensed Materials. If the changes render the Licensed Materials less useful in a material respect to the Subscriber, the Subscriber may within thirty (30) days of such notice treat such changes as a breach of this License under clause 10.1.2 and 10.4.

This section is concerned with the technology platform used to make the product available, and what hardware and software the subscriber will need to access the content. Note that this section has an escape clause, which will allow the subscriber to cancel if any technical changes render the product useless.

The publisher must also:

7.2.2 Use reasonable endeavors to make available the electronic copy of each journal issue in the Licensed Materials within fifteen (15) days of publication of the printed version. In the event that for technical reasons this is not possible for any particular journal, as a matter of course, such journal shall be identified at the time of licensing, together with such reasons.

This paragraph notes when new journal content should be available in the database. No guarantees about content availability are made, however. By using the phrase 'reasonable endeavors', the publisher is protected against a contract violation claim because a journal issue's loading was delayed.

The publisher must:

7.2.3 Provide the Subscriber, within thirty (30) days of the date of this License, with information sufficient to enable the Subscriber to access the Licensed Materials.

This is a standard activation clause, giving the subscriber a timeframe for being able to access the product.

The publisher agrees to:

> 7.2.4 Use reasonable endeavors to ensure that the Server has adequate capacity and bandwidth to support the usage of the Subscriber at a level commensurate with the standards of availability for information services of similar scope operating via the World Wide Web, as such standards evolve from time to time over the term of this License.

This section refers to product performance, or response time, as it relates to the hardware and storage needed to retrieve the content quickly.

Finally, the publisher must:

> 7.2.5 Use reasonable endeavors to make the Licensed Materials available to the Subscriber and to Authorized Users at all times and on a twenty-four hour basis, save for routine maintenance (which shall be notified to the Subscriber in advance wherever possible), and to restore access to the Licensed Materials as soon as possible in the event of an interruption or suspension of the service.

The publisher will, again, use 'reasonable endeavors' to keep the product up and running 24 hours a day, seven days a week.

Product content

The next section indicates that product content can be changed or removed at the information provider's discretion. While most contracts will have language that permits the publisher to remove content, not all of them allow the subscriber to respond. Our sample contract does.

> 7.3 The Publisher reserves the right at any time to withdraw from the Licensed Materials any item or part of an item for which it no longer retains the right to publish, or which it has reasonable grounds to believe infringes copyright or is defamatory, obscene, unlawful or otherwise objectionable. The Publisher shall give written notice to the Subscriber of such withdrawal. If the withdrawal results in the Licensed Materials being no longer useful to the Subscriber, the Subscriber may within thirty (30) days of such notice treat such changes as a breach of this License under clause 10.1.2 and 10.4.

The information provider must be able to remove content and not be in violation of its contract. It may lose the right to distribute a journal because its contract with the publisher was not renegotiated. Or it might discover that an article infringes someone's copyright. In order for the publisher to be able to warrant that it is permitted to offer its product, it has to be able to delete content as necessary. You should read this clause carefully, and make sure you have the right to cancel the contract if critical content is removed. More about negotiating this clause will be discussed in the next chapter.

Archival access

Although post-cancellation access is addressed in section 2.2 of the sample license, it is again discussed, along with archival access, under the 'publisher's undertakings' section. The license states:

> 7.4 The Publisher undertakes to use reasonable endeavors to provide or to make arrangements for a third party to provide an archive of the Licensed Materials for the purposes of long-term preservation of the Licensed Materials, and to permit Authorized Users to access such archive after termination of this License.

Electronic journal archive projects, the third party referred to in this clause, have been established to ensure that journal content is preserved and will be accessible if, for example, a publisher files for bankruptcy or a computer server malfunctions. Long-term preservation of electronic information is of great importance to librarians, and becomes more so as we shift our collection dollars from print to electronic. We used to rely on our print copy for long-term access, since we physically owned the piece. We do not 'own' the electronic version, and so are forced to rely on these third parties to provide long-term preservation and access. The organizations running these archives are charged with storing the content, refreshing it so it remains accurate, reformatting the data as standard access protocols change and making the content available. Some of these journal archive projects also offer post-cancellation access, as mentioned previously, so former subscribers can still use content for which they paid, even if a current subscription is not maintained. Projects developed to provide varying levels of archival access include LOCKSS (lots of copies keep stuff safe) and CLOCKSS (controlled LOCKSS), both of which were initiated by Stanford University; PORTICO, a Mellon Foundation project; and the

National Library of the Netherlands. Although publishers are actively cooperating with one or more of these electronic journal archives, they will rarely specify any third-party archive project in their licenses.

Usage data

The availability of usage data may also be indicated in this section. Standard language concerning the collection and availability of usage data should ensure the anonymity of individual users and confidentiality of the data collected, which our sample license does.

> 7.5 Collection and analysis of data on the usage of the Licensed Materials will assist both the Publisher and the Subscriber to understand the impact of this License. The Publisher shall provide to the Subscriber or facilitate the collection and provision to the Subscriber and the Publisher by the Subscriber of such usage data on the number of articles and of abstracts downloaded, by journal title, on an annual basis for the Publisher's and the Subscriber's private internal use only. Such usage data shall be compiled in a manner consistent with applicable privacy laws, and the anonymity of individual users and the confidentiality of their searches shall be fully protected. In the case that the Publisher assigns its rights to another party under clause 11.3, the Subscriber may at its discretion require the assignee either to keep such usage information confidential or to destroy it.

Standards have been developed for collecting and reporting usage data for electronic products. COUNTER (Counting Online Usage of Networked Electronic Resources), a non-profit entity composed of publishers, libraries and affiliated members, has developed these standards for electronic journals, books and database products. The license may indicate that the information provider is a COUNTER member, and that the usage data offered will be COUNTER-compliant. COUNTER-compliant usage data are discussed in greater depth in Chapter 5.

Liability clause

The term 'liability' means one is subject to a legal obligation, or is responsible. Within an electronic resource license, the liability clause usually lists those events for which the information provider is willing, or not willing, to be responsible, and the limitation of its fiscal responsibility if these events occur. A liability clause will contain language similar to the following:

7.7 EXCEPT AS PROVIDED IN CLAUSE 7.1, UNDER NO CIRCUMSTANCES SHALL THE PUBLISHER BE LIABLE TO THE SUBSCRIBER OR ANY OTHER PERSON, INCLUDING BUT NOT LIMITED TO AUTHORIZED USERS, FOR ANY SPECIAL, EXEMPLARY, INCIDENTAL OR CONSEQUENTIAL DAMAGES OF ANY CHARACTER ARISING OUT OF THE INABILITY TO USE, OR THE USE OF, THE LICENSED MATERIALS. IRRESPECTIVE OF THE CAUSE OR FORM OF ACTION, THE PUBLISHER'S AGGREGATE LIABILITY FOR ANY CLAIMS, LOSSES, OR DAMAGES ARISING OUT OF ANY BREACH OF THIS LICENSE SHALL IN NO CIRCUMSTANCES EXCEED THE FEE PAID BY THE SUBSCRIBER TO THE PUBLISHER UNDER THIS LICENSE IN RESPECT OF THE SUBSCRIPTION

PERIOD DURING WHICH SUCH CLAIM, LOSS OR DAMAGE OCCURRED. THE FOREGOING LIMITATION OF LIABILITY AND EXCLUSION OF CERTAIN DAMAGES SHALL APPLY REGARDLESS OF THE SUCCESS OR EFFECTIVENESS OF OTHER REMEDIES. REGARDLESS OF THE CAUSE OR FORM OF ACTION, THE SUBSCRIBER MAY BRING NO ACTION ARISING FROM THIS LICENSE MORE THAN TWELVE (12) MONTHS AFTER THE CAUSE OF ACTION ARISES.

Liability clauses are relatively simple. Just as we cannot control the behavior of our individual authorized users, an information provider cannot guarantee that a user will not misinterpret or misuse information within its product. In order to protect itself against an individual's lawsuit, filed because the user misunderstood or misused the content, the information provider inserts a clause similar to the one presented above. In some cases, if the subscribing library is part of a state college or university, this clause may have to be modified or deleted, because some state laws prohibit agreeing to a limit in the amount that can be collected if damages are awarded. You should contact the appropriate department on campus to determine if you are permitted to agree to any limitation of liability.

Subscriber's undertakings

In this contract, the subscriber's undertakings refer to the responsibilities the licensing institution has to protect the publisher's content. Here are those clauses discussing the library's responsibilities.

8.1 The Subscriber shall:

8.1.1 Use reasonable endeavors to ensure that all Authorized Users are appropriately notified of the importance of respecting the intellectual property rights in the Licensed Materials and of the sanctions which the Subscriber imposes for failing to do so;

8.1.2 Use reasonable endeavors to notify Authorized Users of the terms and conditions of this License and take steps to protect the Licensed Materials from unauthorized use or other breach of this License.

Notice that these clauses do not indicate how you should convey copyright and appropriate usage information to your users. You should have some mechanism in place (pop-up screen, splash screen, a link to general usage guidelines) to remind users that these materials are copyrighted and their use is governed by individual licensing agreements.

The subscriber must also:

8.1.3 Use reasonable endeavors to monitor compliance and, immediately upon becoming aware of any unauthorized use or other breach, inform the Publisher and take all reasonable and appropriate steps, including disciplinary action, both to ensure that such activity ceases and to prevent any recurrence.

You must be willing to follow through if you detect that someone at your institution is misusing a product. In most instances the information provider will detect unauthorized use, such as systematic downloading or use of a robot that is data mining the product, because it monitors activity on its own servers. It will then notify you, and expect you to address the abuse. A discussion of database breach management can be found in Chapter 2.

The subscriber must:

> 8.1.4 Provide the Publisher, within thirty (30) days of the date of this Agreement, with information sufficient to enable the Publisher to provide access to the Licensed Materials in accordance with its obligation under clause 7.2.3. Should the Subscriber make any significant change to such information, it will notify the Publisher not less than ten (10) days before the change takes effect;

> 8.1.5 Keep full and up-to-date records of all IP addresses and provide the Publisher with details of such additions, deletions or other alterations to such records as are necessary to enable the Publisher to provide Authorized Users with access to the Licensed Materials as contemplated by this License.

While the information provider is required to contact you with the information you need to access the resource, you are required to make sure that it has your institution's current contact information and IP addresses as well.

The library must:

> 8.1.6 Use reasonable endeavors to ensure that only Authorized Users are permitted access to the Licensed Materials.

This is a standard clause reminding the subscriber that it is responsible for limiting access as outlined in the first section of this license, where authorized users are defined.

The negotiator should read this section carefully to make sure s/he is not agreeing to responsibilities that cannot be met.

Words such as 'guarantee' or 'ensure' should be removed and replaced with 'take all reasonable steps' or similar less definite language, thus protecting the subscribing institution while still indicating the institution's commitment to protecting the information provider's content.

Subscriber's indemnity clause

As mentioned earlier, the indemnity clause that appears in the 'publisher's undertakings' section is not the only one in this license agreement. This contract asks the subscriber to indemnify the publisher as well, under certain circumstances.

8.2 SUBJECT TO APPLICABLE LAW, THE SUBSCRIBER AGREES TO INDEMNIFY, DEFEND AND HOLD THE PUBLISHER HARMLESS FROM AND AGAINST ANY LOSS, DAMAGE, COSTS, LIABILITY AND EXPENSES (INCLUDING REASONABLE LEGAL AND PROFESSIONAL FEES) ARISING OUT OF ANY CLAIM OR LEGAL ACTION TAKEN AGAINST THE PUBLISHER RELATED TO OR IN ANY WAY CONNECTED WITH ANY USE OF THE LICENSED MATERIALS BY THE SUBSCRIBER OR AUTHORIZED USERS OR ANY FAILURE BY THE SUBSCRIBER TO PERFORM ITS OBLIGATIONS IN RELATION TO THIS LICENSE, PROVIDED THAT NOTHING IN THIS LICENSE SHALL MAKE THE SUBSCRIBER LIABLE FOR BREACH OF THE TERMS OF THE LICENSE BY ANY AUTHORIZED USER PROVIDED THAT THE SUBSCRIBER DID NOT CAUSE, KNOWINGLY ASSIST OR CONDONE THE CONTINUATION OF SUCH BREACH TO CONTINUE AFTER BECOMING AWARE OF AN ACTUAL BREACH HAVING OCCURRED.

This indemnity clause essentially says that the subscriber is responsible if anything its employees or authorized users do results in a lawsuit being filed against the publisher. If this were the complete content of the clause, however, it would not be acceptable. The language removing liability, or blame, from the library if an individual authorized user is responsible for the misconduct is necessary, because we, as electronic resource contract negotiators, cannot place our institutions in the position of being responsible for the behavior of every student, faculty member and staff member. As long as someone at your college or university, in his/her official capacity, did not help the user commit the violation, and you did not allow the misuse to continue after it was discovered, then your institution is protected. The other positive aspect of the language in the clause is the inclusion of the first phrase, 'subject to applicable law'. If the subscriber is a state college or university, state law may prohibit it from agreeing to an indemnity clause. If that is the case, removing this clause from the contract, while appropriate, would not be necessary, because the clause would not be valid even if it remained in the document.

Indemnity clauses found in other contracts are not nearly as subscriber-friendly. Some do not exempt the subscribing institution from responsibility even if an employee did not cause or perpetuate a contract violation. One such clause reads:

> The Subscriber shall indemnify the Licensor and, where relevant, any third-party information provider or supplier, for any loss or damage suffered arising out of any use of the Information by those Authorized users beyond the rights expressly granted to the Subscriber and/or the Authorized users under this Agreement.

In this clause you are agreeing to pay for any legal fees and damages resulting from use of the product by any authorized user incurred not only by the information provider, but also by its information suppliers. One of your students could post a *New York Times* article on an open website, and that content could be seen by the article's author. The author could then sue the information provider for violating an agreement they had between them. Even though your institution had no involvement in the agreement between the *New York Times* and the information provider, this language would make you responsible for the information provider's legal fees, because your user's behavior violated the terms of your license agreement and precipitated the lawsuit.

Undertakings by both parties

Our sample license has one clause under this heading, stating that both parties agree to respect the 'intellectual property, confidential information and proprietary rights' of the other party. This means that both the publisher and the licensing institution agree to respect the other's copyrights and those rights accompanying ownership of content. And the information provider in particular will protect individual user information, including searches, results and other usage data that can be traced to a single user.

Term and termination

This section of the license may specify the exact length of time the agreement will be in force, and whether or not the license is automatically renewed unless either party cancels the agreement. Also included will be those activities or behaviors that would permit either the information provider or the subscriber to cancel the agreement, as well as the rights and obligations of both parties if the agreement is terminated.

Term of the agreement

The term of an agreement is the period of time for which the subscriber is paying the information provider to access its product. Sometimes the term of a contract will be presented in an appendix, and sometimes it will be an integral part of the contract. In our sample, the term of the agreement is presented at the very beginning of the document. Usually, the term of a contract is one year from the date contained within the agreement. In some cases, however, both the subscriber and the licensor find it useful to negotiate agreements for multiple years – perhaps three or five. In these cases, annual renewal of the agreement is automatic, and the terms of the renewal, such as the amount the subscriber will be obligated to pay for each annual renewal during the contract period, should be defined in an appendix to the contract. Multi-year contracts allow the subscriber to plan ahead and budget accordingly. Licensors may prefer multi-year agreements as well, because they are guaranteed a specific amount of income for the contract period.

Termination

If either signing party does not abide by the responsibilities outlined in the contract, then the information provider should have the right to suspend access to the product, or either party should be allowed to terminate the agreement. The term 'breach' is used frequently in these sections. A *breach* is a violation or infraction, so a breach of a contract is a violation of the terms and conditions outlined in the agreement. A *material breach* is a violation that is so severe that the injured party may consider the agreement null and void, and may pursue damages. Posting of the content of a product on the open web, or not restricting access to authorized users, could both be considered material breaches because these actions have the potential to reduce the commercial value of the product. In such cases the information provider cannot afford to wait until the end of the contract period to cut off access. Termination rights are one way the information provider has to protect its content. The first part of this section in the sample license focuses on what behaviors will allow the information provider to terminate access.

> 10.1.1 If the Subscriber willfully defaults in making payment of the Fee as provided in this License and fails to remedy such default within thirty (30) days of notification in writing by the Publisher.

The first clause is straightforward – if you do not pay, the publisher will cut off access.

> 10.1.2 If the Publisher commits a material or persistent breach of any term of this License and fails to remedy the breach (if capable of remedy) within sixty (60) days of notification in writing by the Subscriber.

This second clause gives the subscriber the right to terminate the agreement if the publisher does not fulfill its responsibilities, and does not rectify the situation as outlined in the contract. Such a breach might be not adding new journal issues within the timeframe outlined in the agreement, and not correcting the omission within the 60 days allotted. The *cure period*, or the amount of time a party has to correct a problem, may be as short as 15 days or as long as 90, although it is usually 30 days. Some licensing agreements do not include such a clause – they focus on the termination rights of the publisher only. But the subscriber should always have the ability to cancel the agreement if the publisher commits a persistent breach.

> 10.1.3 If the Subscriber commits a willful material and persistent breach of the Publisher's copyright or other intellectual property rights or of the provisions of clause 3 in respect of usage rights or of clause 6 in respect of prohibited uses.

The third clause offers the same protection to the publisher that 10.1.2 offers to the subscriber, with an exception. No period to correct the breach is indicated. A reason this language may have been omitted is because the breach would have to be 'a willful material and persistent' breach, rather than a violation that does not put the value of the content in jeopardy. The subscriber, in this case, would have to be aware of the breach and permit it to continue in order to fulfill the requirements of this termination clause. Under such circumstances, the publisher should have the right to cut off access immediately in order to protect its content.

> 10.1.4 If either party becomes insolvent or becomes subject to receivership, liquidation or similar external administration.

The final clause in this section allows either party to cancel the agreement if it becomes bankrupt.

The next three clauses under the 'term and termination' section are concerned with post-termination content management. The first clause specifies that the responsibilities of both parties end when the contract is terminated, except for those related to using the licensed content if post-cancellation access is retained:

> 10.2 On termination all rights and obligations of the parties automatically terminate except for obligations in respect of Licensed Materials to which access continues to be permitted as provided in clause 2.3.

The next clause requires a subscriber which has committed a willful, persistent material breach to stop offering the content to its users immediately upon termination of this contract, except again as permitted under the post-termination clause:

> 10.3 On termination of this License for cause, as specified in clauses 10.1.1 and 10.1.3, the Subscriber shall immediately cease to distribute or make available the Licensed Materials to Authorized Users except as provided in clause 2.3.

If the publisher commits the material breach and the subscriber chooses to end this contract, the final clause specifies that the subscriber will receive a pro-rata refund for the remaining period of the contract. You want to make sure that refund language is in the contract somewhere, either in this section or elsewhere: if it is not included you are not guaranteed to get your money back even if you choose to terminate the contract because the information provider has violated the agreement.

General

The rest of the clauses in the sample license are grouped under the 'general' heading, although the concepts covered in this section could have been assigned their own headings, and often are in other contracts. The type of information covered in this general section varies widely. I will go through the clauses in our sample license briefly, although many of them are self-explanatory.

> 11.1 This License constitutes the entire agreement of the parties and supersedes all prior communications, understandings and agreements relating to the subject matter of this License, whether oral or written.
>
> 11.2 Alterations to this License and to the Schedules to this License are only valid if they are recorded in writing and signed by both parties.

These two clauses refer to the supremacy of this agreement over any prior agreements that may have been signed between the two parties. The first clause may carry the label 'agreement of record'.

> 11.3 This License may not be assigned by either party to any other person or organization, nor may either party sub-contract any of its obligations, except as provided in this License in respect of and the management and operation of the Server, without the prior written consent of the other party, which consent shall not unreasonably be withheld.
>
> 11.4 If rights in all or any part of the Licensed Materials are assigned to another publisher, the Publisher shall use its best endeavors to ensure that the terms and conditions of this License are maintained.

The contract we are discussing is between the publisher and the subscriber, and these clauses reaffirm that. The subscriber is not allowed to sublicense access to this content to another institution, and the publisher cannot subcontract control of the content without informing the subscriber. Of course, another publisher could purchase the journals covered under this agreement, and choose to alter any or all of the terms of use. The current information provider would be unable to prevent this change, or any other alterations to the content, interface or service.

> 11.5 Any notices to be served on either of the parties by the other shall be sent by prepaid recorded delivery or registered post to the address of the addressee as set out in this License or to such other address as notified by either party to the other as its address for service of notices. All such notices shall be deemed to have been received within 14 days of posting.

This language is sometimes contained in a paragraph labeled *notification*. It is included because both parties must be able to contact the other, particularly in the case of a material breach of the contract, and know that the other has received the communication. This is why your account information, as mentioned under section 8 – subscriber's undertakings – must be kept up to date. Fax or e-mail notices may also be permitted, if so indicated in this clause.

> 11.6 Neither party's delay or failure to perform any provision of this License as a result of circumstances beyond its control (including, without limitation, war, strikes, floods, governmental restrictions, power, telecommunications or Internet failures, or damage to or destruction of any network facilities) shall be deemed to be, or to give rise to, a breach of this License.

This is a clause that is often labeled *force majeure* – French for 'greater force'. Essentially, if a force beyond either party's **control** interferes with the fulfillment of either party's responsibilities under this contract, the harmed party may not consider the results of such an event a breach of the contract. For example, if a tornado destroys the building where the publisher's servers are housed, and service is interrupted for weeks while back-up tapes are loaded, the subscriber will not be able to get a refund or pursue any legal remedy.

> 11.7 The invalidity or unenforceability of any provision of this License shall not affect the continuation or enforceability of the remainder of this License.

This clause, protecting the terms of this contract in case any individual clause or section cannot be enforced, may be labeled *validity and waiver of content*. For example, if a state institution cannot agree to indemnify another party, and that clause is determined to be unenforceable, the rest of the contract is still valid.

> 11.8 Either party's waiver, or failure to require performance by the other, of any provision of this License will not affect its full right to require such performance at any subsequent time, or be taken or held to be a waiver of the provision itself.

If one of the participants in this contract does not live up to its obligations, the other party can choose to ignore it. For example, if the contract prohibits using the product to fulfill interlibrary loan requests, and the publisher discovers that the subscribing library has been violating this prohibition, the publisher can choose to cut off access or not. If the publisher chooses the latter option, it does not lose the right to respond to this contract violation in the future.

The last clause under our sample license's general section is a discussion of jurisdiction, or governing law:

> 11.9 This License shall be governed by and construed in accordance with New York law; the parties irrevocably agree that any dispute arising out of or in connection with this License will be subject to and within the jurisdiction of the courts of New York.

Jurisdiction specifies the geographic region whose legal entity will interpret the terms and conditions of the license. The original contract will list a state, a county or even a country where any disputes arising from the contract will be heard. Usually the jurisdiction reflects the location of the information provider's offices, giving its attorneys a legal advantage, as they are most familiar with their own state's laws. The subscriber's attorney may not be familiar with that state's laws, and would be forced physically to attend court out of state, a potentially costly undertaking. To protect your institution from the cost and inconvenience of a distant jurisdiction, you should automatically change the jurisdiction to your own state. A more thorough discussion of the issues surrounding a contract's jurisdiction appears in the next chapter.

Another clause that may be found in licenses, although not present in our sample agreement, is a *confidentiality* clause. The inclusion of such a clause compels the subscriber to keep confidential either the legal terms of the contract, or the business terms (how much you are paying), or both. One confidentiality clause reads:

> The subscriber agrees that it will not use or disclose information relating to this license or the business terms and conditions set out therein. The licensor may

terminate this agreement if there is a breach of this confidentiality clause.

Such a clause may be included because an information provider does not have an established price list for its products and services, or it may have drastically altered the terms and conditions of an agreement for a particularly skillful negotiator. Information providers would prefer that such contract terms do not become general knowledge, or they may be compelled to offer similar pricing and licensing terms to all their customers. In some instances, advertising the prices paid for databases may not be in a subscriber's best interest either. For some state institutions, particularly those whose states have broad freedom of information policies, signing a contract containing a confidentiality clause may not be permitted. Some private institutions may not be able to agree to the language either, if they are required to disclose this type of information to any external entities, such as a board of trustees.

Signatory lines

Each agreement should have signatory lines for both the information provider's and the subscribing institution's representatives. The latter person may be the license negotiator, the library's head of collections or the dean. Or those authorized to sign contracts on behalf of the institution may be outside the library – in the institution's attorney's office, or in business services. Whoever signs the contract must have the authority to do so, or the contract itself becomes invalid. Prior to the signatures, a license may contain a sentence that states this very need: 'In witness to the above agreement, those below warrant that they are authorized to sign this agreement on behalf of their respective entities.' Thus, before signing any agreement, the license negotiator should determine if he/she is authorized to commit the institution legally to the terms of any contract. If someone in the library is permitted to sign on behalf of the college or university as a whole, then the library's dean or another high-level administrator should sign all the agreements, in order to shift contract enforcement responsibilities to someone who has a stronger standing within the institutional hierarchy.

I have not included every clause found in every contract in this discussion. Some licenses may be one paragraph, others as long as 20 pages. Discussing all the possible permutations found among electronic resource licenses is not possible, but the sections discussed above are some of the most common. If any section or clause of the contract does not make sense, ask your information provider's representative for clarification, or discuss the language with your institution's attorney. Do not agree to any language you do not understand. You may be restricting how your institution or authorized users can use a product, or you may be committing your institution to behaviors or actions that are, in reality, impossible to perform. The next chapter will cover strategies to help you modify standard contract language in order to protect your institution and make the terms and conditions more suitable for your users.

4

Successfully negotiating an agreement

The information provider has a resource and your collection managers have decided they want to offer access to this resource to your users. Two things often stand in the way of completing a successful negotiation: the license and the price. Working with the information provider to remove these obstacles is the goal of the negotiation process. Learning how to negotiate is an art as well as a science. Most of us have been in a position to negotiate something – we may perhaps have haggled over the price of a car, a house or a bike at a yard sale. And most people would admit that they dislike negotiating, or believe they are not very good at the process. A number of books have been written on how to negotiate successfully, both in business situations and within personal relationships. If you are not confident of your ability to work your way through the negotiation process, one of these books may be of interest. The classic text addressing this issue is *Getting to Yes* by Roger Fisher and William Ury. Although originally written in 1981, this book remains relevant, as the basics behind reaching an agreement between any two parties have not changed. This chapter will not attempt to duplicate the contents of this or any other books that address developing negotiation strategies. Rather, it will focus on the specific issues inherent in the library/information provider conversation. The issues that might arise during licensing and pricing negotiations will be discussed, and suggestions offered to help resolve them.

Entering into the conversation with the information provider with the right attitude is the first step toward a successful negotiation. Unfortunately, some library negotiators approach this process with a negative or even belligerent attitude. Working with information providers is viewed as an 'us versus them' encounter. They assume that conflict is inherent in the process. This need not be the case. The tension between librarians and publishers seems to be a recent phenomenon, traced back to the serials' crisis of the late 1980s. During this period, serials' price increases exceeded the cost of inflation over a number of years. A number of academic and scientific societies chose to have commercial publishers manage the production and distribution of their journals. And static library budgets led to wide-scale journal cancellations. This crisis has never really gone away – librarians have compensated by shifting costs to interlibrary loan and document delivery services, to continue providing access to journal articles without maintaining costly subscriptions. The protracted issues tied to journal pricing in higher education have librarians questioning publishers' motives, and have encouraged the development of commercial publication alternatives. But the truth of the matter is that for-profit journal publishers still control most of the market, and they are not going away in the near future.

Understanding the motives behind the publisher's position in the negotiation process will help you understand this position and allow you to move forward with your negotiation. There are some important points to remember.

■ The publisher's goal is the same as yours – to make its content available to your researchers. It is not successful if you choose not to license with it.

- The information provider's representative assigned to your institution will not, as a rule, have the power or position within the company to make any decisions. The publisher's representative is playing the role of communications conduit, as you may be within your organization. S/he relays your issues and concerns to those who can make decisions on behalf of the company, and then communicates those decisions to you. Understanding the representative's role can help alleviate tension that might exist between you and the representative, because s/he, ultimately, is not responsible for whatever decisions are made. Of course, some representatives may be unable or unwilling to communicate the library's concerns; or sometimes a company's internal lines of communication may not function well. If such a situation exists, contacting your representative's supervisor or the regional manager is the best way to proceed.

- The commercial publisher is in business to make money. Although to many this is obvious, we sometimes forget that publicly held publishing companies have a responsibility to their shareholders to show a profit. The intrusion of the commercial world into the world of the non-profit educational institution can create tension, but it is the nature of the business. You may not agree with the amount of profit these companies make, but that issue should not prohibit you from entering into discussions with a company – unless your selectors and/or library administration have decided to boycott certain publishers because of their business practices.

- As a practical matter, some companies have policies or practices that make them difficult to work with. Draconian licensing terms and unreasonable inflation rates are part of the licensing experience. Your greatest negotiation strength in such a case is your ability to walk away. Many of us have been in a situation where we were forced to agree to terms and conditions with which we were uncomfortable, because we did not have the ultimate authority to say no. Depending on your position within your institution, you may or may not have that authority to walk away from a negotiation. If you can, then you will be in a position of strength. If, however, you are not the person who makes the final decision concerning the value of a certain product to your institution, you should not advertise this situation. If the information provider knows or believes you *must* have the product it is offering, it will be less willing to negotiate.

By keeping these points in mind, your interaction with the information provider's representative can be more pleasant and productive. The value of a long-term, congenial relationship with a company and its representatives is immeasurable.

Negotiating licensing terms

The previous chapter discussed common sections, clauses and terms found in an electronic resource licensing agreement. This chapter will go through the same sample license, and highlight those areas where conflict may arise between you and the information provider. The reasons behind these conflicts will be explored, as will options for language changes that should satisfy your institutional needs as well as the needs of the licensor.

Key definitions

Authorized users

For academic institutions, faculty, staff and students must be permitted to access the licensed resource, and these constituencies are almost always included in the 'authorized users' definition. But in some situations, walk-in users or members of the public who are not affiliated with the college or university may not be permitted to use the resource. This type of restriction may be in place because the product was designed and priced originally for a non-academic market. Many of these databases are then licensed to academic institutions, but at a greatly reduced price. The information provider may believe, rightly or not, that public access to this product through your library competes with its ability to license the same product to for-profit customers. Publishers are concerned that potential customers will choose to send their employees to your library rather than licensing the resource themselves. Not surprisingly, business and law information companies commonly restrict walk-in access.

The first step in negotiating walk-in access is determining if you really need it, or if you can limit access to the product to institutional affiliates only. If your library is closed to the public, this is not an issue. Even if your library is open to area residents, you may determine that walk-in access to this specific product is not necessary. To comply with the license restriction, however, the technological infrastructure must be in place to restrict access to this product. Most libraries now require some form of authentication to access their computer network, even within their buildings, but some do not have this protection. If you cannot prevent walk-ins from accessing your databases, then you must either include them in your license as authorized users or not license the product.

If you have decided that you want to or must provide walk-in access, your next step is convincing the information provider to allow you to do so. Although its primary concern about walk-in use is a loss in commercial licensing revenue, the information provider may also be concerned that it could be liable if a member of the public misuses a product or misunderstands the content, and as a result files a lawsuit against the publisher. The latter concern is easily remedied. You could suggest it adds an introductory click-through screen to the product, forcing the user to absolve the company from any liability based upon how the product is used. The former concern is more difficult to allay. The question is, would for-profit companies in your area have subscribed to the product in the first place? Walk-in clients who are employees of businesses in your area may be using your institution's resources rather than licensing them directly. But to use the product, these patrons must come to your facility – they would not be able to use the resource from their offices. This inconvenience alone is enough for larger organizations to justify their own subscriptions. And smaller business owners would probably never unilaterally license a product they might use only occasionally.

Another reason walk-in access should not affect a company's income is the prevalence of business resources available through other venues, such as the internet and the area's public libraries. In fact, your public library may already offer access to resources with similar information. Some state libraries license business-related resources, because they support business growth and economic development. Such products may be made available through public and school libraries across the state. With all these resources available, a local business owner is unlikely to license a database unless the content is critical to the company's success.

Authorized sites

Although not as prevalent as they were in the past, highly restrictive site definitions still appear, usually in licenses for individual journal titles. Such a clause may limit access to a single geographic site, defined either by the distance from the library (a five-mile radius is common) or as a series of architectural structures. While our sample license does not contain a site definition, a clause that restricts access based on geography would be:

> For the purposes of this license, an institution is defined as one contiguous campus community and network, including any halls of residence of faculty, staff or students; or, in the commercial sector, e.g. pharmaceutical companies, one contiguous commercial office complex.

Language restricting access in this manner is most likely included to allow publishers to maintain their income levels as distribution of content shifts from print to electronic access. Not surprisingly, despite the format shift some publishers continue to manage their electronic subscriptions as they did their print subscriptions. In the print world, every location that had a need for a certain journal's content would maintain a print subscription. The problem with translating the print model to the electronic environment is that all physical locations in an organization, which are tied together through their telecommunications infrastructure, would not have wanted or needed print access to this content, but will now have electronic access. And a site license will require them to pay for this content, just because they cannot be excluded from access technologically. For example, a university may have multiple branches around a geographic region, or even a state, and each location may offer unique academic programs. But because IP addresses for this institution are intermingled across the system, no single location can be isolated. This means that any electronic journal would be accessible to all locations, even though the vast majority of use would come from a single location. Another flaw in imposing a restrictive site definition is the availability of remote access. Our clientele expect to be able to access electronic products not just from a library, but also from their offices, off-campus apartments and homes, many of which may fall outside the defined geographic parameters. If remote access is not permitted, much of the appeal electronic journals hold is removed. But if remote access is permitted, there is no logic in imposing a site restriction in the first place.

The information provider may have no idea how restrictive its language is for academic institutions. Many licenses were developed for commercial customers, with little thought given to the academic market. Just raising the issue may be enough to have the site definition removed from the contract. If the content of the single journal or portfolio of titles is highly specialized, odds are that the audience for these publications is very small, and these users are located in the same department or college. Therefore, as mentioned earlier, providing access to multiple locations will probably not result in a dramatic increase in use, because only one site actually needs access to the content. In the print environment your institution would have held only one subscription to the title, so providing access to an entire organization at the single subscription price allows the publisher to maintain its income level while giving broad access to the content.

Also supporting the elimination of the site definition is the inclusion of an authorized user definition. This definition, ensuring that only people affiliated with the subscribing institution will have access to the product's content, may also convince the publisher. Where these authorized users are located should not be an issue, particularly if remote access is already permitted.

If the information provider would prefer not to remove the site definition altogether, because it does not want a state university system such as the State University of New York (SUNY) to pay the same price as a single institution, you might consider offering an alternative definition. One such site definition takes into account institutions with multiple geographic sites, provided these sites are managed centrally:

> An authorized site may be an institution located at a single geographic site, or may be an institution with locations at multiple geographic locations, as long as these locations are all administered centrally from the licensing location.

Only a multi-site institution could comply with this definition; a state university system or a consortium could not, because each institution within such an organization is an independent entity.

The rest of the definitions offered in our sample license are commonly used, and should not require any negotiation. But you need to read these definitions carefully, because they will determine how those terms are used later in the document.

Agreement

The only issue in this section that might create the need for negotiation is post-cancellation access. Some publishers offer it, others do not. If it is offered, the contract should specify how that access will be provided. It could be through the publisher's interface, through a third-party provider, or in the form of a CD-ROM or other physical format. If you want post-cancellation access to journal content, and it is not offered in the license, then you need to add language similar to that found in the sample license. And if you want that access in a particular format or through a specific interface, you also need to specify this in the added language. Of course, for some products, like indexing and abstracting services, requesting post-cancellation access is illogical and it will probably not be granted.

Usage rights

As discussed earlier, when we subscribe to print journals we are permitted, under copyright law, to make certain uses of the articles within those journals. But if the license prohibits these uses, we no longer retain those rights granted to us under US copyright law. Our sample license specifies the permissions granted to the subscribing institution under the heading 'subscriber's rights', and those given to individual users under 'authorized users' rights'. This is a logical division because copyright law is organized in a similar manner, distinguishing between the rights of an individual and those of a library or archive.

Our sample license is an excellent example of a contract that provides those rights an institution would like to retain – specifically interlibrary loan and electronic reserves. In fact, the subscribing institution retains all rights granted to it under copyright law, which is ideal. Adding language similar to clause 3.3 to all your contracts will eliminate the need to add individual clauses specifying each right provided for under section 108 of the copyright law.

The 'authorized users' rights' section is more restrictive, although it is still a good model. Some basic permissions that should always be given under this section include searching, viewing, retrieving and downloading search results, and saving, printing and distributing articles or portions of the product to authorized users. Without some of these basic rights, this product would be of little use to our constituents. And, inevitably, our users would violate the contract because they would have to perform these activities in order to make use of the product. Ideally, you would want to retain an individual's ability to use a licensed work as he or she is permitted to do under copyright law. To accomplish this, you could modify the language in clause 3.3 of our sample license to read: 'Nothing in this License shall in any way exclude, modify or affect any of the Subscriber's *or Authorized Users'* statutory rights under US copyright law.'

Interlibrary loan

Although articulated separately in the sample license, interlibrary loan, electronic reserves and course pack permissions are usually placed under 'usage rights'. As mentioned earlier, contract language frequently found in electronic journal licenses states that interlibrary loan is permitted if the electronic article is printed, then sent to the receiving library through a fax-like service called Ariel. This process degrades the image three times – once when printed, again when it is scanned and yet again when printed at the receiving library. While laborious, this seems to be the protocol which makes publishers most comfortable.

Electronic reserves

Electronic reserves utilizing an electronic journal subscription are not as much of an issue if the publisher's software is capable of generating a stable URL or a direct link to the journal article. Linking to content is not considered a violation of copyright and is seldom prohibited in a license, although in rare cases a product may not technologically support linking to the article level.

Scholarly sharing

Scholarly sharing means just what it says – one researcher sharing relevant content with a research colleague from a non-profit institution which does not license that resource. While our sample license does not include a clause permitting this type of use, you may want to add such a clause to your agreement. The language may require the user with access to the content to print out the material and mail it to the colleague, rather than allowing the electronic file to be shared.

The challenge in negotiating the 'usage rights' section, as well as others, is to understand the concerns of the publisher and find a middle ground that will permit you to use the resource in the manner you require while protecting the publisher's content. Ask for the inclusion of language that will allow you to use the digital version of the content as you would have used the print version under copyright law. You may be required to transform the digital version back into print in order to exercise these rights. Although you will then not be able to take full advantage of the rapidity and flexibility offered by the digital format, you will not lose any of the rights that you had under copyright law, and you will still be able to provide the same level of service as with the print incarnation of the work.

Prohibited uses

Rarely would you want to add anything to the two sections under this heading, since you are probably not interested in restricting further how a product may be used on your campus. The prohibited activities in the sample license are reasonable. But again, read this section carefully, and if you believe your institution or users need to have the ability to use a product in a manner that is prohibited, remove the clause, add those rights to the 'usage rights' section, and be prepared to defend your request to use the product in that manner.

Publisher's undertakings

There are two clauses under this heading of our sample license that might raise issues during the negotiation of an agreement: the indemnity and the notification of content change clauses.

Indemnity clauses

Indemnity clauses can contain among the most confusing and difficult language to manage. As mentioned in the previous chapter, if you indemnify someone, you agree to be responsible for legal fees and any fines, damages or other costs, under certain circumstances outlined in your contract. The ideal indemnity clause is one that has the publisher indemnifying you from a third-party lawsuit precipitated just because you are using the product. Again, the language in our sample license reads:

> THE PUBLISHER SHALL INDEMNIFY AND HOLD THE SUBSCRIBER HARMLESS FROM AND AGAINST ANY LOSS, DAMAGE, COSTS, LIABILITY AND EXPENSES (INCLUDING REASONABLE LEGAL AND PROFESSIONAL FEES) ARISING OUT OF ANY LEGAL ACTION TAKEN AGAINST THE SUBSCRIBER CLAIMING ACTUAL OR ALLEGED

INFRINGEMENT OF SUCH RIGHTS. THIS INDEMNITY SHALL SURVIVE THE TERMINATION OF THIS LICENSE FOR ANY REASON. THIS INDEMNITY SHALL NOT APPLY IF THE SUBSCRIBER HAS AMENDED THE LICENSED MATERIALS IN ANY WAY NOT PERMITTED BY THIS LICENSE.

If this language is not already part of the agreement, you may want to consider adding it. Since the publisher must warrant, or guarantee, that it has the right to offer the service in the first place, it should always indemnify you against any third-party claims.

If at all possible you do not want to indemnify the publisher, and you never should indemnify the publisher against the actions of a third party. For example, let us say the information provider infringes the copyright of a third party, such as offering access to a journal article without the author's permission. If you have agreed to indemnify the company against third-party claims, your college or university would be legally obligated to pay for the information provider's legal fees, as well as any court judgments made against the publisher, even though your institution played no role in the infringement. The following clause, or any clause with similar language, should be struck out of a contract:

The subscriber shall indemnify the publisher and, where relevant, *any third party information provider or supplier* for any loss or damage suffered arising out of any use of the information by authorized users, beyond the rights expressly granted to the subscriber and/or the authorized users under this agreement. [Emphasis added.]

Not only are you being asked to indemnify the publisher in this clause, but if you do not alter or remove this language you will also be responsible for indemnifying third parties – people who are not even part of this contract. You could find yourself paying for multiple legal actions because a user's activity resulted in legal action against the information provider and its content supplier. Your first step would be to remove this clause in its entirety. Many state institutions are prohibited from indemnifying a contractual partner against the claims of an individual or organization that is not a direct participant in the contract. If you are licensing for a state institution and this is your state's law, then this language must be removed from the contract. Negotiators for private institutions should still remove the clause to protect their college or university, although they might encounter resistance on the part of the information provider.

Sometimes the publisher is not willing to indemnify you unilaterally. If you are allowed to do so under your state's law, you might consider mutual indemnification. Such a clause would require your institution to pay the publisher's legal expenses if it suffered harm because one of your employees committed a material breach of the contract, helped someone else breach the contract or knew about such an activity and did nothing to stop it. A mutual indemnity clause would contain the same requirements for the publisher. It would have to pay your court costs if one of its employee's actions resulted in your institution being sued. A mutual indemnification clause looks like the following:

> The licensor shall defend, indemnify and hold the subscriber harmless from and against any and all liability, loss, expense (including reasonable attorneys' fees), or claims for injury or damages arising out of the performance of this agreement but only in proportion

to and to the extent such liability, loss, expense, attorneys' fees, or claims for injury or damages are caused by or result from the negligent or intentional acts or omissions of the licensor and its employees.

The subscriber shall defend, indemnify and hold the licensor harmless from and against any and all liability, loss, expense (including reasonable attorneys' fees), or claims for injury or damages arising out of the performance of this agreement but only in proportion to and to the extent such liability, loss, expense, attorneys' fees, or claims for injury or damages are caused by or result from the negligent or intentional acts or omissions of the subscriber and its employees.

The goal of the indemnity clause is to have the party responsible for any behavior that harms the other party pay for any legal fees that result from this misbehavior. The problem for libraries is that they are licensing on behalf of their entire college or university population, which for some research institutions is over 50,000 individuals. It is impossible for any single department, like the library, to monitor the behavior of all these people. And certainly, no institution should be willing to take financial and legal responsibility for the behavior of each individual affiliated with it. You should read every indemnity clause carefully, to guarantee that you do not make your institution responsible for every student, faculty member, staff member and walk-in user who accesses a database. One way to shift the responsibility back to the individual is to include language that specifically protects the institution. Our sample license includes a clause that provides this protection:

NOTHING IN THIS LICENSE SHALL MAKE THE SUBSCRIBER LIABLE FOR THE BREACH OF THE

TERMS OF THE LICENSE BY ANY AUTHORIZED USER, PROVIDED THAT THE SUBSCRIBER DID NOT CAUSE, KNOWINGLY ASSIST, OR CONDONE THE CONTINUATION OF SUCH BREACH AFTER BECOMING AWARE OF AN ACTUAL BREACH HAVING OCCURRED.

Even if you agree to a mutual indemnification clause, you may want to include this or similar language, just for clarification. If one of your users unilaterally misuses the content of this product in such a way that it harms the publisher, the publisher will have to recover legal fees and damages from the individual user.

Notification of content change/reimbursements

No product content is completely stable. Publishers sell and purchase journal titles all the time. Aggregators also lose and gain full-text journal content. The product you originally agreed to license may very well not contain the same information when you consider renewing at the end of the license term. In some cases a library may choose to license a database because that product contains a certain title or set of titles, although this content comprises only a small portion of the total product. If that content is removed from the database, the subscriber deserves to know, and should have the opportunity to cancel the agreement. This is the logic behind the notification clause. The information provider, on the other hand, may find the logistics of agreeing to such language daunting. Tracking the losses and gains of entire journal titles is not difficult. But for those managing an aggregator product, guaranteeing subscriber notification of not just the loss or gain of whole titles but specific issues and years of different titles could be an issue. Those of us who have implemented an open URL resolver product are aware that companies offering aggregated full-text products may not know the entirety of their products' content at any given time – we often receive complaints when an article that should be available is not there. Because an aggregator licenses its content from various publishers, its ability to retain content depends upon these publishers renewing their distribution agreements. Managing the status of these agreements and communicating this information among the offices that license aggregated content, load content into the product and interact with customers are complex undertakings, and inevitably mistakes will be made.

That being said, the company providing the content should have the internal structure in place to notify subscribers of content changes, at least at regular intervals, such as monthly or even weekly, and this requirement should be articulated under publisher responsibilities in the license agreement. Any language added to a contract requiring notification, however, should also include an escape clause, based upon changes to the product's content. Such a clause would allow the subscriber to cancel without penalty, and would grant a refund of the amount corresponding to the time remaining on the contract. The specifications of such a clause can differ among licenses. One clause may permit the subscriber to cancel and request a refund if any change in content is made to the product. Such language is contained within our sample license. Another clause, which may be preferable to information providers, focuses solely on the amount of content removed from the product, as compared to the total product:

> The licensee agrees to notify the subscriber of any change to the product's content. If the amount of content lost equals ten (10) per cent of the total

product content, the subscriber may choose to cancel this agreement and receive a pro rata refund.

This language allows the information provider to focus just on the volume of lost content. If, rather than losing total content, the publisher swaps access to one journal for access to another, it has not lost content volume and the escape clause would not be applicable. Of course, the lost journal may have been critical to a subscriber, but this language would not permit a mid-contract cancellation. You will need to determine whether including this language is appropriate for the product you are licensing. In some cases, such as a publisher-based journal package, you most likely will not be able to negotiate a blanket content-loss clause, because publishers lose and gain titles frequently. You may, however, be able to negotiate the inclusion of a volume-loss clause, in case the publisher loses the rights to a number of journal titles and does not gain any new titles to add to its portfolio.

Subscriber's undertakings

No changes to specific clauses are recommended in this section of our sample license. But you need to make sure you do not agree to any term or condition with which you or your institution will not be able to comply. In this spirit, you want to replace any word that requires an absolute response (must, have to, guarantee) with words that give you some flexibility (attempt to, make all reasonable efforts, best endeavors). For example, you cannot guarantee to restrict access to authorized users only; but you can use all reasonable efforts to restrict access to authorized users. Remember the adage that 'promises are meant to be broken': do not make a promise in a contract that you may, knowingly or unknowingly, break.

Term and termination

The key negotiating point in this section is the addition of a cure period. The publisher is granted a 60-day period during which it is permitted to cure a breach in the contract before the subscriber can consider the contract voided. What is missing, however, is a period of time that will allow you to fix a breach committed by you or your users. Under this agreement, the publisher can cut off access immediately if a willful, material and persistent breach occurs, compromising its product. If a user is systematically downloading the entire contents available from a publisher, then yes, I would agree to an immediate cessation of access in order to protect the publisher's property. But language should be added that gives the subscriber an opportunity to fix the problem before access is permanently terminated.

Jurisdiction

Subscribers probably request changes to this section more frequently than any other. Both the subscriber and the information provider want to have their state's or country's law governing the terms and conditions of the agreement, in case any legal action is brought against either party. Most state institutions will be required to change the jurisdiction to their own state for all contracts. This requirement is not for convenience only; contract jurisdiction has implications associated with the state's right to claim sovereign immunity. Sovereign immunity is a 'judicial doctrine that prevents the government or its political subdivisions, departments, and agencies from being sued without its consent' (Phelps and Lehman, 2004, Vol. 9: 255). This protection is codified in the Eleventh Amendment to the US Constitution, which prevents citizens from other states or countries from filing lawsuits against a state entity. As we know, electronic resource licenses are entered into voluntarily. If a representative of a state agency agrees to a contract in which the jurisdiction is outside the state, some believe this could be considered a voluntary waiver of the state's protection under the Eleventh Amendment.

Some information providers, particularly those located overseas, may refuse to accept the governing law of the subscriber's state. In such a situation, if state law or institutional policy permits, the subscriber can eliminate the jurisdiction clause entirely. Remaining silent on the jurisdiction is controversial, because if one of the parties pursues legal action, an additional hearing must be held so a court can determine what law will govern the terms and conditions of the agreement. This additional hearing will, of course, cost both parties time and money. When making its decision, the court will consider 'what the parties intended as to which law should govern; the place where the contract was entered into; and the place of performance of the contract' (ibid., Vol. 3: 169). Thus the final decision is unknown. Those who support the option of remaining silent on the jurisdiction are not as concerned about these issues, perhaps because legal action focusing on contract terms between licensors and subscribers is extremely rare.

Information providers, for the most part, understand that those of us who work for state institutions must either change the jurisdiction to reflect the state where our institution is located or remove the clause altogether. The former is preferable for the subscriber, because it guarantees that its state law will be in control. The second option – removing the clause altogether – means that a judge will decide which jurisdiction will prevail, resulting in an additional court hearing and additional costs to both parties. Including a clause that would require both parties to go to arbitration (see below) makes logical sense if both parties are permitted to do so. Again, some state institutions will not permit their agencies to submit to arbitration, because they are concerned about losing their sovereign immunity rights and legal flexibility. In these situations, little negotiation can be done. State law has to be followed, and the library negotiator should indicate this to the information provider's representative.

Arbitration

Arbitration is defined in *West's Encyclopedia of American Law* as 'the submission of a dispute to an unbiased third person designated by the parties to the controversy, who agree in advance to comply with the award – a decision to be issued after a hearing at which both parties have an opportunity to be heard' (ibid., Vol. 1: 326). An arbitration clause may already be a part of some jurisdiction sections of a contract. This section will most likely indicate who or what company will perform the arbitration, and where that arbitration will take place. A common arbitration clause states:

> The parties to this agreement irrevocably agree that each and every controversy or claim arising out of, in connection with, or relating to this agreement or the interpretation, performance or breach of this agreement shall be settled by arbitration in the city of New York, NY, in accordance with the arbitration rules then established by the American Arbitration Association or its successor.

The next section continues by stating that arbitration must be attempted prior to either party taking legal action. The same problem of physical location exists for the subscriber.

An institutional representative would have to travel to the arbitration site, and incur all the costs associated with such travel. And, again, some states will not allow their agencies to agree to binding arbitration, because it limits the state's legal options.

Uniform Computer Information Transactions Act

Some jurisdictions are more consumer-friendly than others. Jurisdictions to be avoided include Maryland and Virginia, both of which have passed the Uniform Computer Information Transactions Act (UCITA). UCITA is designed to create legal consistency across all states, focusing on software licensing, information access and information technology transfer. UCITA is not a law that can be passed at the federal level – like the Uniform Commercial Code, each state's legislature must approve it individually, because the states control the laws governing commercial transactions within their jurisdictions. Uniform codes attempt to harmonize these laws across the country, to facilitate commerce among different states. The result of UCITA's passage, in very general terms, is that consumer protection against onerous contractual obligations has been reduced. No other states have passed UCITA, and it is not pending in any state legislatures at this time. You should be aware, however, that this legislation still lingers, and should not agree to any state's jurisdiction where it has been approved.

Negotiating business terms

Business terms are those parts of the license that determine when an agreement will begin, how long the subscription period is, what the renewal terms are and how much the institution will pay for access. These elements are often negotiable, some more readily than others.

Start date/duration of agreement

In my experience, libraries tend to treat an electronic resource subscription start date more like a monographic purchase than a serial. Rather than beginning or cancelling a subscription on the calendar year, as we usually do for print journal titles, we begin offering access to a database on the date when the contract agreement is processed, which could be any day in any month of the year. That means we have products with renewal dates occurring throughout the fiscal year, creating difficulties when managing our institution's electronic resource portfolio. One option is to manage your license terms so the majority of your subscriptions expire at the end of the calendar year. Should you add product access at any other time during the year, you might consider requesting a pro-rata term for the first year, so your renewal date will fall on 1 January. If your institution has a large number of subscriptions, you might consider clustering renewals to distribute the workload across the year.

The duration of the agreement can mean two things. The first is the duration of the business terms, or how long you agree to pay the current amount. Business terms are usually in effect for one year. This allows the information provider to adjust the price of its product annually, just as print publishers tend to do. With an annual renewal, the terms of the license will usually continue to be in effect, even though the business terms change. Our sample contract offers an agreement in which the terms and conditions of the license do not have an expiration date, but the content being licensed is specified. This information is conveyed through a schedule, which appears at the end of the contract. Schedule 1 indicates that the content being licensed is published in 2008. If the subscriber wishes to continue subscribing in 2009 it would have to sign a new Schedule 1, but would not have to renegotiate the terms and conditions of the license itself.

An information provider may be willing to offer an agreement with business terms that extend across multiple years. Either the company will offer a single price that will remain constant over the life of the agreement, or it will establish a level of inflation that will be applied annually to the price of the product. Information providers see the value of a multi-year agreement for two reasons: they have a guaranteed income from your institution for the life of the agreement, and they do not have to process paperwork every year, which saves staff time. Subscribers may also find a multi-year arrangement appealing, particularly for products that are used heavily. Budget planning for the next fiscal year is easier if the cost of a number of information resources is already determined. Staff time managing these titles is also reduced. If a multi-year agreement is entered into, you should consider adding an escape clause in the license, just in case your institution's fiscal situation changes dramatically. Our sample license has language in section 10.1.4 that allows either party to terminate the contract if it goes bankrupt. Because a college or university is not likely to go bankrupt, this language is not very helpful, but it can be altered to include the possibility of dramatic library collection budget cuts. Because higher education funding levels are not guaranteed, some states require the inclusion of a budget-triggered escape clause in all multi-year licenses. A funding contingency clause would resemble the following:

> In the event the Subscriber's state legislature or central administration appropriates or budgets insufficient funds for payments due under this contract, the Subscriber will immediately notify the Licensor, and this contract shall terminate on the last day of the subscription period for which payment has been made without penalty to the Subscriber. In the event of such termination the Subscriber shall maintain its perpetual rights to materials licensed during the subscription periods for which it has fully paid.[1]

If you work for a state college or university, your institution's attorney or purchasing office may have language available that you can insert into any multi-year agreement.

Duration of the agreement can also mean the length of time the licensing terms and conditions are in place. Some colleges and universities want to review each license every year, while others prefer to have the terms and conditions remain in effect indefinitely. The former practice may be of value for those institutions with small collections, and which have a streamlined purchasing process. The latter is the norm, and is certainly more efficient. If a product's license requires renegotiation annually, you might consider requesting that the duration of the licensing terms be extended.

Renewal process

Gathering all of the information necessary to make a renewal decision can be a challenge. One critical piece of data, the renewal price, can be surprisingly difficult to obtain. A contract might require the subscriber to give up to three months' notice if it plans not to renew a product, but the information provider will rarely have a renewal price available that early. To ensure that you have all the information you need to make this decision, the contract should include a clause requiring the information provider to submit the renewal price far enough in advance of the deadline for a renewal decision such that you, your fellow librarians and teaching faculty have the opportunity to discuss the renewal. Modifying the section of the license that outlines the renewal timetable will accomplish this. Replacing a renewal clause that requires a decision two or three months prior to the product's renewal date with the following language should be sufficient: 'The subscriber has 30 days from the date of the receipt of the renewal invoice to notify the licensee of the decision to renew or cancel.' Even if the information provider is late in sending an invoice, and the product is scheduled to expire before the end of the 30 days, you would still be able to cancel without penalty. This encourages the information provider to send a renewal invoice in a timely fashion, and gives you ample time to consult with interested parties and make an informed decision.

Pricing

Pricing, for most subscribers, is the element of the business terms and conditions that creates the most concern. In some cases an information provider will have a pricing policy or published price list based upon institutional characteristics or a formula. The benefit of a published price list is knowing what the costs will be before initiating contract negotiations.

In some cases product pricing is not negotiable. Most companies, however, have established a framework within which they determine pricing, taking into account one or more features or characteristics of the subscribing institution. But the exact price they charge an individual institution is not prescribed. This section will review various pricing models information providers currently utilize, and options the negotiator might consider if the asking price does not accurately reflect the value of the product to the subscribing institution.

FTE-based pricing

FTE, or full-time equivalent, is a way to measure enrollments. Two half-time students are equivalent to one full-time student, or FTE. Sometimes this figure is reported in total – undergraduate, graduate and professional school students – and in some cases graduate or professional FTEs are separated from undergraduates. This is one model that allows the information provider to differentiate between the very small and the very large institution, and price its products accordingly. General databases and aggregated full-text products are often priced based on FTE bands. This model works well for those products that have broad appeal, because it takes into account the overall user population and thus reflects the value to the subscribing institution.

FTE pricing does not work as well, however, when the subject or scope of the product is more focused. Institutions with a large number of students will pay a disproportionately larger amount for a product that a relatively small number of students and faculty will use. And in some cases the same number of potential users may be found at a very large research university and at a smaller, more specialized college, but the larger institution will pay substantially more. One approach to negotiating FTE-based pricing for a more specialized product is to look at the number of users who fit a specific profile and will be more likely to use the product. For example, you may be interested in licensing a highly specialized mathematics product. The publisher wants to charge you $50,000 for the product because your institution is very large, with around 50,000 students. But, because the product is so specialized, your potential user population consists only of the graduate students in math, numbering 50 students. Based on the actual user population, as opposed to the total student population, you may be able to negotiate a greatly reduced price, perhaps $1,000 a year. This approach to pricing does not literally restrict access based upon department; it acknowledges that the product will be available to all authorized users, but only a small portion of the subscribing institution's population will find the product useful. The cost truly reflects the value of the product to your institution. Many information resource companies that license highly specialized products understand that there is limited interest in their resource, and may be willing to agree to a reduced FTE count as the basis of their pricing, upon your request. A challenge to this pricing strategy is determining which populations should be counted. Currently no standards exist to help us define 'science' FTEs, for example, because so many disciplines are interconnected. If this is an approach of interest to you and the information provider, make sure you agree upon what populations will be counted.

Concurrent-user or seat-based pricing

The other pricing model information providers use most frequently is based upon the number of users from an institution who will be able to access the product simultaneously. This model literally limits concurrent access. For those products that have a limited user population, concurrent-user pricing is a logical alternative to FTE-based pricing. Surprisingly, even at a very large institution, the number of users who will try to access a single product at the same time is fairly small. Because of this, the seat-based model makes financial sense for a larger institution that wants to offer access to a greater number of specialized products at the most economical price. Some information providers will try to require larger institutions to license a greater number of seats. Again, as with FTE pricing, requesting the number of concurrent users based upon the appropriate population is the suggested strategy to employ when you negotiate pricing.

Concurrent-user-based pricing raises some unique management issues that may or may not reduce the attractiveness of this model. Turnaways are the first concern. Turnaways are the people who attempt to access the resource while all of your seats are in use. To help you manage the product, the information provider should be able to supply turnaway counts on a monthly basis. Having actual turnaway data will allow you to determine whether the number of seats you have licensed sufficiently accommodates user demand. When renewing your agreement, you should have the option to increase or decrease your seats accordingly.

The message your users see when all your seats are occupied is the second issue. These messages can be cryptic – providing little or no information about the actual status of the product. The user may assume that a technical problem exists, and give up rather than trying the product again at a later time. Knowing what this message says allows you and your technical support staff to be prepared for the inevitable questions. If a turnaway message is too cryptic or discourages use, you should contact the information provider and request that it changes the message to convey the actual status of the product.

A third challenge created by seat-based pricing is in library instruction. Because the number of users who can access a resource at the same time is limited, teaching these resources during a hands-on library instruction session can be an issue. Not all participants will be able to practice with the product at the same time. The instruction librarian can choose to demonstrate the product personally, and not have the students follow along concurrently, or members of the class can alternate accessing the product. The most efficient answer to this challenge is to contact the information provider and request additional seats for the day of the class. All information providers should be willing to increase your concurrent-user access, or provide ID/password access to a different account that permits an unlimited number of users, for the duration of the class. This solution, of course, requires planning, as the information provider's technical staff will need time to accommodate your request. While the user or seat-based pricing model requires more attention to monitor and manage than others, for some products with a limited audience this approach to pricing allows you to provide an appropriate level of access to a resource of limited interest at a reasonable price.

Single-user ID/password pricing

Some information providers offer single-user pricing only. This may be because the publisher primarily works with individual subscribers, and not with libraries or larger institutions; or it may not be able to manage access to its product based on anything other than an ID/password.

If this is the case, then negotiating pricing for this product may depend upon how you want, or are able, to provide secure access. Some libraries keep a list of ID/passwords at a service desk and have staff members log users into these resources, or library staff hand out the information to users upon request. In some cases the ID/password-protected product's access is further limited, because the user must log in from a specific computer – remote access is not an option. Because user access to these products is highly limited, the cost of an institutional subscription should reflect this. Some products do not limit access to one specific computer, so users may log in from any location. To manage these ID/passwords, some libraries maintain a password-protected website that lists ID/passwords for these resources. Subscription costs for such products may be higher, because the number of people able to access the resource at the same time is greater. The most efficient way to manage a resource that requires an ID/password is by scripting the needed information. This involves creating a program that will automatically enter the ID/password when a user clicks on a link. In order to regulate access to the product, users are forced through the institution's proxy server, requiring everyone to authenticate before accessing any content. A library should never create a script to log into an information provider's product without explicit permission. You may be asked to pay more than list price for a resource to which you have created scripted access, as you have expanded access to your entire institution. Such broad access was probably not envisioned when the product's pricing structure was originally developed. (One note: you should be notified immediately if the information provider changes or resets either the ID or the password, so you can update your own access information or change your script.

Language requiring notification of these or any access protocol changes should be included in the contract.)

Carnegie classification

A few information providers use an institution's Carnegie classification to determine pricing for their products. The Carnegie Classification of Institutions of Higher Education is a structure that organizes all accredited, degree-granting institutions of higher education. The classification matrix groups institutions based on, among other criteria, enrollment, student selectivity, degrees granted and research productivity. Basing pricing on Carnegie classification takes into account the number and level of graduate programs offered, as well as the amount of research conducted at the institution. The amount and sophistication of undergraduate research are very different to that which occurs at the graduate and faculty levels. Pricing based on Carnegie classification reflects this difference. But the classification of the institution as a whole may not reflect the level of use a specific product will receive. Your institution may be a research university with a very high research volume, but the product you want to license may support a program which offers only a master's-level degree. In this case, you should attempt to negotiate a price reduction to reflect the level of research occurring in the program that the product will support.

Online journal pricing

Electronic journal pricing models can be complicated, because they are usually based upon some combination of print subscriptions, online access and, perhaps, the bundling of additional, unsubscribed titles. In the early days of electronic journals, the focus was on the individual title. Publishers offered free online access with a print subscription, or charged a nominal fee. As the popularity of the electronic incarnation of these titles increased, the value of the print subscription diminished. Most online journal subscriptions are now content-based rather than print-based – meaning that the journal's content is the basis for the bulk of the cost, not the physical journal itself. The pricing model has essentially been reversed. Print has become the add-on, available for an additional fee. This fee is usually a percentage of the full subscription cost; journal subscription agents refer to this as deep discount pricing, or DDP. Many libraries have given up their print subscriptions entirely, saving not just money but also staff processing time, binding costs and storage space.

Pricing for an individual journal title is usually not negotiable, for two reasons. First, publishers issue catalogs with price lists. Secondly, most libraries work through journal subscription agents, which primarily handle print subscriptions but have begun to manage some electronic subscriptions as well. These companies manage thousands of journal subscriptions for thousands of different libraries. If each library has a different pricing agreement for each individual journal title with each journal publisher, subscription agents would be unable to manage any institution's journal portfolio.

The same cannot be said for large journal package agreements. Whether managed through a subscription agent or directly with the publisher, complete publisher-based journal packages do not have set pricing. You can negotiate various elements of the package's cost, in part because of the large dollar value and title count each package represents. For a larger library, the monetary value of these packages can be hundreds of thousands of dollars. In most cases the base cost of the journal content is the stable element, meaning that the published title subscription price is the one upon which the rest of the costs are built. For example, if you want to retain a print subscription to some of the journals you may be able to negotiate the cost, which could be anywhere from 6 to 25 per cent of the journal's content cost. Many publishers offer libraries an incentive to sign multi-year agreements – three or five years are standard contract lengths. In these agreements the publisher will offer a fixed inflation rate for the life of the agreement. This percentage can also be negotiated. Finally, some publishers offer the option to license access to their entire title list, not just those titles the library selects. This is known as the 'Big Deal'.[2] An additional cost, sometimes known as a top-up fee, is added to the value of those titles to which the institution originally subscribed. This cost might be a percentage of the selected journals' value or it could be a flat rate, and it can usually be negotiated. Table 4.1 illustrates the costs that might be associated with a multi-year journal package agreement.

Negotiating these costs is done on a case-by-case and publisher-by-publisher basis. Many of these agreements contain confidentiality clauses, restricting the subscribing institution's ability to share the business terms with colleagues, so you may have difficulty finding out the terms other institutions have successfully negotiated.

Published price lists

Some information providers do not use a model to determine the pricing of their resources. They have published price lists, and do not waiver from those prices, except perhaps at the end of the sales quarter or fiscal year. If your sales representative is trying to meet her goal for the

Table 4.1 Sample pricing model for a publisher's journal package

Cost for e-only titles	100% of catalog price
Cost for print plus online access	115% of catalog price
(savings for going e-only 0% of catalog price)	
(deep discount cost for print 15% of catalog price)	
Top-up fee for access to entire portfolio	15% of library's current expenditure
Inflation rate for five-year agreement	4.5% annually
If the library's current expenditure on this publisher's titles, prior to this agreement, was $100,000, then the figures would be:	
E-only content costs	$100,000
Cost to retain print for all titles	$15,000
Top-up fee for access to all titles	$15,000
Annual inflation rate – add 4.5% to total cost every year for the next five years.	

month, you might be able to negotiate a reasonable discount. Also, these representatives are aware that librarians will frequently choose to license products that have a one-time cost at the end of the fiscal year, in order to acquire new content, spend out their budgets and carry over continuing funds to the next fiscal year. Information providers may be willing to accept a reasonable price for a product, even if that amount is lower than the published price. If you have only $25,000 available to buy a $35,000 product, make an offer.

Comparing prices among third-party information providers

In some cases, databases may be available from multiple companies. These third parties provide the interface and manage the subscriptions on behalf of the entity that owns the content. An example would be EconLit. Although the American Economic Association (AEA) owns the content contained within the database, the database itself is made available through a variety of interfaces, including EBSCOhost, Ovid SilverPlatter, CSA Illumina and OCLC FirstSearch. The AEA charges each of these third-party providers the same amount for access to its content. These companies then add a further charge, or royalty, covering their technical and management costs and, of course, their profit. The royalty differs from company to company, and the amount they charge their customers will also vary depending on how each calculates its fee. Obtaining quotes from appropriate third-party companies and using that information to negotiate access with your preferred provider is an excellent strategy to get the content you need at the best price possible.

Conclusion

The bottom line, when negotiating the license or price for an electronic resource, is to approach the conversation in a reasonable fashion. First and foremost, be honest about who will have access to the product and how you will provide that access. If your institution has multiple locations, and the contract prohibits this, negotiate the authorized site definition. Do not assume that the information provider will never know that you are going to use a product in a manner the contract prohibits. Just as librarians like to share their experiences with information providers, information providers talk with each other as well. Also remember that information providers and librarians are not enemies. Ultimately, our goal is the same. We both want our users to have access to a product. Determine what a reasonable cost for the product would be, based on the relative costs of other similar products and the amount of use such a product is likely to get on your campus, then work with the information provider's representative to come to a mutually satisfactory arrangement.

Notes

1. This language is based upon the funding contingency clause contained within the standard license agreement used by the Regents of the University of California. Their model document is available at www.cdlib.org/vendors/CDLModelLicense.rtf.
2. The phrase the 'Big Deal' was originally coined by Kenneth Frazier (2001), director of libraries for the University of Wisconsin, Madison, in an article in *D-Lib Magazine*.

5

Selecting and managing titles in your electronic resources portfolio

Managing your electronic resources is as critical, if not more so, than the licensing process. Libraries are devoting more and more of their fiscal resources to serials and serial-like products. Even many of those electronic resources for which we pay a one-time fee require an additional annual maintenance or interface fee. With more funds being devoted to ongoing costs, libraries are reducing the number of books they are able to purchase. And once an electronic resource is licensed, librarians find it very easy to continue to renew them – not scrutinizing them annually as we do with our print journal subscriptions. This chapter will offer some suggestions on selecting an interface, when you have an option, tracking usage of these products once you license them and reviewing the products for renewal or cancellation. But because electronic resources and collections are managed differently in every college and university, the specifics offered in this chapter might not translate well to your organization, although you may find the broad concepts useful.

Selecting electronic resources

How do you decide if your institution should have access to a certain resource? Your current print collection and your curriculum should provide ample guidance.

What do you have in print?

If you are considering an electronic information product, the logical place to begin is with your print collection, particularly your reference and serials titles. These types of resources lend themselves well to the digital environment for several reasons.

■ *They are most useful if they can be searched across issues/volumes.* The electronic version, particularly of a print index, saves the user time and aggravation, because the entire index can be searched at once. In the print environment the user has to search each annual volume individually.

■ *They are easier to use in electronic form.* Journals, indexes and other reference works can be difficult to locate and use in their print incarnations. Many users have difficulty locating journals in their library's online catalog, let alone tracking down the physical piece in the stacks. Some print reference works – citation indexes, for example – require users to consult multiple volumes in order to find the information they need. The electronic iterations of these products are easy to locate, and much easier to use than their print counterparts.

■ *They are used by a wide audience.* Reference works in particular are of interest to a broad constituency. From undergraduates through faculty, all have from time to time a need for the basic information contained in a variety of reference materials.

- *They are not read in their entirety.* We all know that reading a large amount of text on a computer screen can be difficult. Reference works are consulted to answer specific questions. Journal articles are scanned to determine their relevance to the researcher's question, and those of interest are usually printed for later consultation.

- *They have ongoing costs associated with them.* Journals are paid annually via a subscription, and reference works may either come out annually or be superseded by newer editions. In either case, the library usually has continuing funds earmarked for the print product, so little if any additional funding should be required to shift formats.

- *They take up a great deal of shelf space.* Most titles that are received in a serial fashion will eventually take up a large amount of shelf space. Shifting these titles to an electronic format will alleviate the staff and facility costs associated with material shelving and storage, both in your current stack areas and in your remote storage facility.

- *They support your institution's face-to-face and online reference services.* Having your reference collection available electronically greatly facilitates your library colleagues' ability to offer reference services. If you have multiple reference desks, you no longer need to purchase multiple subscriptions of basic reference tools if you subscribe to them electronically. And if your library has an electronic reference service, because your reference tools are available online, your librarians can respond to questions when they are in their office, on the reference desk or even at home.

For these reasons, reference resources and journals are highly appropriate titles to focus on when building your electronic resources portfolio.

What other products will support teaching and research on your campus?

While reference resources and journals are a practical place to begin developing your electronic resources collection, a myriad of other product types are available electronically, including historic collections and books. Providing access to the digital version of these resources enhances their accessibility and usability. For the researcher who studies rare or fragile materials, having those resources available electronically, and within an interface that accommodates sophisticated searching, creates vast new research opportunities. Requests to license these resources will most likely originate with your subject faculty, who may have heard about these products from colleagues or previewed them at a conference. Of course, availability of funds will be a major factor in determining whether you can provide access to these products. Almost all information providers are willing to set up trials to assist you and your users in evaluating the value of their products.

Selecting your database provider

While most of the content available through licensed electronic resources is proprietary, or the property of a single company or entity, some products can be accessed through a variety of different interfaces, as mentioned in the previous chapter. Full-text electronic journal articles may be available directly from a publisher's website and also through an electronic index/journal aggregation product, such as ProQuest Research Library or EBSCOhost Academic Search Premier. These aggregator databases, and many other subject-specific databases, not only index a broad variety of journals, but also offer some full-text access. Journal publishers make the decision to permit one or several companies with aggregator products to use their content, but these same publishers may also choose to remove their content at any time, within the terms of their contract with the database provider. The challenge for librarians is keeping abreast of the availability of full-text titles in this ever-changing environment, and deciding whether or not to depend on aggregator database products to provide full-text journal coverage.

Journal articles are not the only content available from a variety of different sources – indexing and abstracting services are as well. While many products are available from only one service provider and through only one interface, other products may be available through a number of different third-party interface providers. Those most frequently found in academic institutions are EBSCOhost, ProQuest, CSA Illumina (owned by ProQuest Information and Learning), OCLC FirstSearch, Gale InfoTrac and OVID. Each of these interfaces offers a variety of different user experiences. While users may start their search using a simple 'Google box' keyword search, more sophisticated searching options, as well as other interface features, are part of almost every electronic resource interface. Librarians will need to discuss those features that are a high priority to themselves and their users, and make their supplier decisions based upon these needs. Some of the functionalities users and librarians want from these interfaces are listed below.

- Simple and advanced search options, which allow the combining of terms using Boolean operators (and, or, not, etc.).

- A journal title browsing option, if full-text journals are included in the product.

- The ability to search specific fields within individual records, such as title, author, source and descriptors.

- Limit options, including date, publication type, language and target audience.

- Search history options that can be saved and retrieved.

- Alert services that notify the user when records corresponding to an established profile are added to the database.

- A thesaurus that allows the user to 'explode' or narrow the search based upon a structured language hierarchy.

- The ability to search across products licensed from the same company.

Some of these functionalities are interface-based, and some, such as a thesaurus, are content-based. Other functions may be desired, depending upon the subject and content of the product.

Cost will also play a role in interface selection, as will an institution's historical preference for a certain company. Some libraries license the majority of their products from the same company, because they always have. The justification for remaining with this provider may include reduced preparation time for bibliographic instruction and a reduced number of interfaces for students to learn. Balancing the desire to have a variety of functionalities, interface familiarity and fiscal constraints is a challenge you and your collection managers will need to address.

Open URL/federated-search-compliant products

Another consideration is whether an interface, or any other product for that matter, is compatible with external services that your library may consider acquiring. A number of companies have developed open URL resolvers and federated search products, but in order to be of any value they must be compatible with the electronic resources you have licensed.

Open URL resolvers

An open URL resolver is a product that links your indexing and abstracting services to full-text electronic journals and books. When a user conducts a search in a database, the open URL resolver receives various pieces of metadata from that database, identifying the requested article. Some of the information transmitted includes the journal title, ISSN, author, article title, publication date, journal volume, issue number, pages and DOIs (digital object identifiers). In order to create the link between this database and full-text content, however, the database must be open URL compliant, or able to generate an open URL that is readable by the open URL resolver. Those that are compliant are known as 'sources'. Almost all major information providers are open URL compliant, although some work more effectively than others. Many smaller company interfaces are not able to generate an open URL request or receive one. Open URL compliance may play a role in determining what products you choose to add to your electronic resources portfolio. The full-text product that contains the journal article you are seeking is known as the 'target', and must also be configured to interpret the metadata request from the source. Targets include aggregated full-text databases, publisher journal packages and individual journal and book titles. A large number of full-text journals are open URL compliant, and thus accessible through an open URL resolver.

Federated search products

A federated search product facilitates searching across multiple products, licensed from different information providers, at the same time. While the searching functionality is not as sophisticated as that available through a product's native interface, a federated search engine allows the novice searcher to see, in a general fashion, what the literature on a certain topic looks like. Currently there are two primary federated search products: Ex Libris's Metalib and WebFeat. These companies sell the software that allows the subscribing library to configure and manage its databases to permit cross-searching, but they are not responsible for establishing the protocol that enables an interface to be cross-searched. That programming is the responsibility of the database provider. Because federated searching is still a relatively new service, many products are not able to be configured and thus cannot be cross-searched. If your library has a federated search product, whether a database is cross-searchable or is in the process of becoming cross-searchable may be another factor you consider when determining which electronic resource products or interfaces to license.

MARC records

An electronic resource may seem valuable upon first glance, but if your users are not aware that it contains specific kinds of information, then your collection dollars were wasted. This is a particular concern when we license a database containing an amalgam of content. Could our students and faculty guess that a product labeled SpringerLink, for example, contains full-text journals as well as electronic books published by SpringerVerlag? Would they even know that Springer was the publisher of the book or journal they are seeking? Or would a user, based on the product's title, have any idea what types of publications a product like ECCO (Eighteenth Century Collections Online) contains? No single title could convey the breadth of information available in either of these collections. But we want our faculty and students to make use of these products, because the content is valuable and we have invested a large amount of money to acquire them. One of the best awareness tools available remains the online catalog, where our students and faculty still search for books and other types of information. When you consider purchasing a product that contains collections or individual book and journal titles, you should ask if MARC records, or pre-configured catalog records, are available. Preferably these would be full MARC records, not just skeletal records that have no subject information included. Subject access is important, because that is how many of our users will 'discover' some of the treasures buried within a large electronic product. MARC records may be free, or may cost an additional fee. But without MARC records, your users' ability to find this information will be limited, which is why their availability is a factor when evaluating such a product.

Product accessibility

Not all of our students or faculty members are able to read a computer screen, limiting their ability to use our electronic resources. We, as advocates for our users, need to encourage all electronic resource providers to make their products accessible to those researchers with disabilities. This may mean that a text-only version of the product is available, and can be read with text-to-speech software. Product accessibility, or the publisher's commitment to developing an accessible version, may be a selection criterion for your library.

Reliability of the product and stability of the company

Of major concern when licensing a product is whether the website hosting the resource is reliable, and whether the company providing the information is financially stable. Both these issues can play a role in the reliability of a product. While you cannot control the availability of a database, you can guarantee either an extension of the contract or a refund if the product does not meet performance standards defined in the contract. But that is of little help at a time when the product is down and your users are attempting to access the resource – which inevitably happens at the height of the semester or during an instruction session. A company's reputation for offering stable, uninterrupted access to its products should be a selection criterion, particularly if the resource is available through multiple platforms. If a company begins to have consistent issues with the stability of its servers, this may be a reason to switch providers or cancel access altogether.

Rarely do information providers go out of business, but they do merge on a regular basis. Before selecting a product and signing an agreement, you will want to know what will happen to your agreement with a company if it no longer offers the product, is no longer in business or is purchased by another company. Again, the contract should cover these contingencies, ensuring that you will have the right to a pro-rata refund if the company no longer offers the product. If the company declares bankruptcy, however, you will most likely never receive a refund. Larger information providers are stable companies, and although there have been a number of mergers in the past few years, the acquiring companies have consistently retained a product's original interface and identity, at least for a reasonable period, allowing the subscribing institutions to transition smoothly. If, however, you are not happy with the results of a merger, you should seek alternative sources for the information you are licensing.

Managing your licensed resources

Once you have selected your provider, then effectively negotiated the licensing agreement, you now have to manage the product. This can be a complex undertaking, particularly for those whose institutions have a large and diverse electronic resources portfolio, because each product and every information provider is different, with different licensing terms, interfaces and technical support protocols. Although electronic resources management requires a fair amount of technical knowledge and is complex and time-consuming, rarely do libraries devote enough staff members to the task. Management becomes more of a challenge because it often falls to the same person who negotiates the agreements also to handle technical support and other related responsibilities.

Technical support

You will need to set up a mechanism by which your users can contact someone within the library when they experience difficulty accessing a resource. Most institutions have multiple avenues through which users contact library staff. General 'help' e-mail addresses or websites are used, as are e-mailboxes specifically established for electronic resources support. Some users may contact the library through a virtual reference site. Others still use the telephone. The challenge for the library is to establish a triage system, so that users' questions are reviewed internally, sent to the appropriate person and responded to in a timely fashion.

A parallel support option is to develop a frequently asked questions (FAQ) website for both internal uses: to assist library staff in answering basic access questions and for your user community. Such a document will help in answering common questions, and save staff time for more complicated queries or those that require contact with the information provider. Table 5.1 shows an example of a database-access troubleshooting FAQ, adapted from Penn State's FAQ. An FAQ is useful only if it is easily located and kept up to date – otherwise it will not be used, or will generate more questions and create confusion.

A crucial step in resolving a technical support question is determining where the problem lies. Is it with the user, the user's internet service provider, the information provider's servers or the library's computer system? If the problem is with the user, is her computer configuration incorrect or is his user ID/password incorrect or expired? You first need to determine where the user is – if she is on campus or off. If she is off campus, and you can access the resource from on campus, then the problem is not with the information provider. At this point you will need to know what error message the user is receiving, which may offer some insight into the problem. It may be with the user's computer configuration. While you cannot know the computer requirements for every product you license, you should know some of the consistent, basic requirements, such as those outlined in the sample FAQ. The problem may also be with the library's proxy server, since the remote user needs to go through the proxy in order to authenticate. Or the user may not be properly registered with the university, which means the proxy server does not recognize him/her as an authorized user. Learning what questions to ask and which problems occur most frequently takes time and practice, but with experience troubleshooting will become easier. Work with the information provider's technical support people, who deal with access

Table 5.1 Sample database troubleshooting FAQ

Authentication problems If you are trying to access a database from outside the Large University network, you will be prompted for an ID/password. If you are denied access after entering this information, it might be for one of the following reasons. ■ The password is case-sensitive. Check to make sure your caps lock is not engaged on your keyboard. ■ You mistyped either your ID or your password. ■ When you created your access account password, you used all numbers instead of an alpha-numeric combination. You should establish a new password with the University's Computer Support ID department. ■ Your ID/password has expired, or you are no longer considered an authorized Large University user. Please contact the Registrar's office to re-establish authorized status.
Browser configuration If you are able to authenticate but cannot access a database, the problem could be caused by your browser configuration. Please check the following. ■ You have metatags enabled (in Internet Explorer). ■ For many of the databases we license, you need to have Netscape version 6 or higher or IE version 5.5 or higher. ■ Your browser is equipped with 128-bit encryption. You can check your cipher level by going your browser's Help option. It will tell you what level of encryption or cipher you have. If it is below 128, you need to upgrade your browser. ■ You have cookies enabled. ■ You have Java Scripts enabled.
Computer platform Some of our databases may not be designed to interface with Macs in the same manner as they interface with PCs. If you are using a Mac and experiencing technical problems, please contact the Information Resources helpdesk directly, if possible. The product's technical staff will be able to assist you more quickly that we can, as the Libraries' technical support staff are most familiar with the Windows operating system.

Table 5.1 Sample database troubleshooting FAQ *(Cont'd)*

Log-in prompt on campus If you are trying to access a database from a dormitory or office, and are prompted to log into the system, please notify us at er_help@largeu.edu and let us know what your IP address is. We may have to work with the service provider to resolve this problem.
Bookmarks or accessing an electronic resource directly If you are trying to access a database directly or through a bookmark, without going through the University Libraries A–Z list, you will be unable to do so from off campus, and in some cases you will not be able to access them via the University's network. When accessing any University Libraries database, please access it through the University Libraries website at www.library.largeu.edu/scripts/databases&subtab=all.
Course management system If you are establishing a course management system site, please use the links provided by the Libraries in your toolbox. Again, your students will be unable to access these databases or electronic resources remotely if you link to the database directly rather than utilizing the Libraries' links.
Printing problems If you are unable to print a document from a database, the problems will more than likely be caused by your printing configuration or be with the vendor. If you receive a page not found or 'access denied' message, please notify us at er_help@largeu.edu. We will need to know what database you are using and the citation of the article you are trying to retrieve.

issues frequently. They may be able to offer assistance, particularly if you cannot determine where the problem lies. They will be more than happy to help resolve the problem if they can, or at least help narrow down potential causes.

Electronic resource management systems

Managing electronic resources is not only about troubleshooting technical problems. It also encompasses the internal management of licensing terms and conditions, business terms and product costs and renewals. When libraries licensed only a dozen products, maintaining paper files with this information was the norm, and not terribly burdensome to library staff. But now, with some libraries licensing hundreds of databases, journal packages, individual journal titles and electronic books, maintaining paper files has become onerous. A number of libraries began to develop in-house databases to track critical pieces of information about each product. Some are simple access databases, while others are highly sophisticated products, such as those developed by the Colorado Alliance (Gold Rush) and Johns Hopkins University (HERMES). A number of companies saw the market for a commercial product that would replace these home-grown databases, and the accompanying miles of paper licenses stored in filing cabinets. These companies include Ex Libris (Verde), Innovative Interfaces (Millennium), VTLS (Verify) and Serials Solutions (360 Resource Manager). Guiding the development of standards for these products was a working group put together under the auspices of the Digital Library Federation (DLF). The goal was to 'develop common specifications and tools for managing the license agreements, related administrative information, and internal processes associated with collections of licensed electronic resources' (Digital Library Federation, 2004). Such a product would provide a single location where both library staff and users could locate information about each electronic resource, including trial information, acquisitions costs, review and renewal information and licensing terms and conditions. The benefits of such a resource are tremendous. Interlibrary loan and electronic reserves staff can refer to the electronic resource management system to see if they are permitted to use an electronic journal for reserve or interlibrary lending purposes. Selectors can find renewal and pricing information, and administrative IDs and passwords which will allow them to access usage data. The size of your electronic resources portfolio, the complexity of your library or library system and available finances will all play a role in determining whether your institution acquires such a product. But as libraries continue to allocate their collections budgets to license electronic resources of all kinds, the need to manage these complicated agreements and products will become more acute.

Evaluating/reviewing/cancelling electronic resources

Because electronic resources are easy to use, available 24 hours a day, seven days a week, and accessible from on and off campus, they become part of the research culture of an institution. Students, faculty and librarians become acclimatized to certain products and services, and have no desire to lose access to any of them. Also, at least in some of the libraries with which I am familiar, electronic resources funding is centralized; because central funds cover inflation for these products, no individual selector has an incentive to review or cancel them. Print journals, on the other hand, are continuously reviewed, and titles cancelled to cover the cost of inflation or to add new titles. There are various reasons why many libraries have not established an annual review process for their electronic resource subscriptions, as they have for their print journal and index subscriptions. But as budgets remain static and our subscription costs increase, money is shifted from monographic purchases to cover inflation, unless subscriptions are cancelled. Decades of journal review projects have reduced our print serials to core titles – leaving electronic resources as the only area where cancellations offer the opportunity to see true savings. Because many people across multiple disciplines use these resources, representatives from a number of constituencies should be involved in a coordinated effort to gather input, evaluate usage and make retention and cancellation decisions. The larger the institution, the more complex this process can become, because a greater number of people have an interest in the fate of each product. The rest of this chapter outlines just one way you might consider conducting an electronic resource review project.

Establish a committee

I know establishing a committee is how we make all our decisions. But in this case, a committee with representation from a broad variety of subject areas will ensure that your review process is inclusive and without bias, real or perceived, toward any subject area. Committee membership should include someone from each discipline (social sciences, humanities, sciences, etc.). Selectors within these groups should be responsible for appointing a review committee representative. Committee members should have a broad knowledge of their field, and the ability to work with those selectors they represent. Individual subject selectors should solicit and aggregate student and faculty input when appropriate. Inclusiveness gives the committee and the process legitimacy. Smaller organizations will not need to establish as complex a communication structure as this, but should still establish a representative committee to review all electronic products.

Compile a list of licensed electronic resources

Creating such a list is another obvious step, but it can be more complex than it first appears. Although many of us maintain a public list of databases for our users, this list may not include individual journal titles, books, encyclopedias or other reference works that you have cataloged and made available through your online catalog only. Your public list may also not include non-networked titles or those that are available only from a single workstation. Inclusion of these products in the review process is a local decision, although the responsibility for individual journal titles and stand-alone products should ultimately lie with the subject specialist. Other pieces of information you may consider including in your list are product costs over the past two or three years, noting the inflation rate; whether this cost is an access fee (for those titles where your institution has purchased the content outright) or a subscription fee; the product's subject area; renewal month; name of the information provider and/or publisher; concurrent-user limits (if applicable); and any other restrictions or relevant information concerning the subscription. Having this information available in one document will facilitate the review process.

Compare content

A library may license multiple aggregated indexing and abstracting services – both general and subject-specific – which contain full-text journal content. If this same library licenses a number of aggregator products from the same company, the odds are that the full-text content in these products overlaps substantially. This same library may also license full-text journal packages and individual electronic journal titles. Inevitably, among all of these resources, journal content is duplicated. Although time-consuming, comparing the full-text content in your electronic subscriptions could show that the relative value of one product with little unique content is much lower than the value of another product. Information providers should be willing to supply a title list for their products, and some will even have documents comparing their products to those of their competitors. You might also be able to use an open URL resolver or serials management product to see which databases offer access to the same full-text journal title, and what years of that title are available.

Gather usage data

In order to help you and your subject collection development librarians monitor the use of an electronic resource, you should have access to vendor-provided usage data. Until relatively recently, this information was provided in a variety of forms and formats. No two sets of data from two different companies recorded the same activities or were offered in the same format. Frustration resulted, because data that do not correspond to the same type of use cannot be compared between and among databases. In 2002, to address the chaos surrounding information resources usage data, an initiative called COUNTER (Counting Online Usage of Networked Electronic Resources) began.[1] Now a non-profit organization based in England, COUNTER has established different sets of usage-data-reporting protocols for journals, databases, e-books and reference works. Journal and database reports record the following usage.

- *Journal Report 1* – Number of successful full-text article requests by month and journal.

- *Journal Report 2* – Turnaways by month and journal.
- *Database Report 1* – Total searches and sessions by month and database.
- *Database Report 2* – Turnaways by month and database.
- *Database Report 3* – Total searches and sessions by month and service.

Reports that a COUNTER-compliant information provider may supply, but is not required to provide, are as follows.

- *Journal Report 1a* – Number of successful full-text article requests from an archive by month and journal.
- *Journal Report 3* – Number of successful item requests and turnaways by month, journal and page type.
- *Journal Report 4* – Total searches run by month and service.

The COUNTER code of practice that addresses usage data for books and reference works includes the following reports.

- *Book Report 1* – Number of successful title requests by month and title.
- *Book Report 2* – Number of successful section requests by month and title.
- *Book Report 3* – Number of turnaways by month and title.
- *Book Report 4* – Number of turnaways by month and service.
- *Book Report 5* – Total searches and sessions by month and title.
- *Book Report 6* – Total searches and sessions by month and service.

In both these sets of reports, 'service' refers to the collection of information which can be licensed and searched through a single company, such as Cambridge Scientific or SpringerLink. These report categories now make it possible to compare the usage of two electronic journals accurately, even if different publishers or host sites offer access to the titles.

While information providers are offering usage data to their subscribers in a more consistent and comparable fashion, getting that information to your subject specialists can be a challenge. This is because most usage data are made available through product administrative modules protected by IDs and passwords, or are sent in a monthly e-mail to the product's local administrator. Neither reporting protocol makes accessing and disseminating usage data easy. One way to address this issue is to assign someone to gather usage data every month and post them on an internal website. This aggregates all usage data in one place, rather than requiring selectors to know how to navigate each product's administrative module. Realizing how time- and labor-intensive such a process would be, MPS Technologies developed a product called ScholarlyStats (recently acquired by Swets), and more recently Serials Solutions has released 360 Counter. Both products pull usage data from the information provider and provide access in a uniform interface. While useful for those resources whose companies participate, neither of these products will ever provide a one-stop shop for usage data management.

Usage data can be a helpful tool in determining the value of a product to your user community. Just looking at raw usage data, however, does not offer useful information, because products and services covering different types of information and different subject areas will be used in very different ways. One product supporting a subject area with a large user population might get much higher use than another, but the latter product may be the only resource in a subject area. And the product that receives less overall use may not cost very much, or may serve a small yet politically influential faculty.

One objective way to compare the relative value of two products that serve different constituencies and cost different amounts is to determine the annual cost per use. This cost is calculated by dividing the number of accesses or downloads into the annual cost of the product. If, for example, you pay $450 for a journal, and that journal had 670 full-text downloads during a year, the cost per download would be 67 cents. Another journal that costs only $100 a year, but had just 20 downloads during that same year, would have an annual cost per use of $5 – a significant difference. But cost per use still should not be the only factor considered when comparing the relative value of products. Subject selectors, who know their disciplines as well as department faculty and their research interests, should be directly involved in any collections decision, no matter what the product's format.

Another factor that will skew your usage data is the implementation of a federated search product. These products enable librarians and individual users to set up groups of products that can be searched simultaneously. Each of these searches will be tracked and reported as a specific kind of search, as defined through COUNTER. This does not mean, however, that the search was appropriate for that product, or that the user retrieved any valuable results. Thus the number of searches recorded for products included in database groups will frequently exceed the number of searches for more esoteric products, or those products that are not able to be cross-searched through a federated search engine. But the quantity of searching done within a database does not necessarily correspond with the quality of the product or the value of that product to your users.

Rank products within subject groupings

Having gathered all this information about your subscribed titles, you may choose to rank them in order of relative value. If your collection is large, I suggest that you do this within each broad subject category, rather than ranking the entire collection as a whole. This again ensures that no single subject area takes the brunt of the cancellations – unless, of course, your college or university has downsized or discontinued a program. The ranking could just be in order of importance, or you may consider grouping your rankings into categories such as core titles; important, but not core; and potentially expendable. (Note: if this is the route your subject selectors choose, you may need to instruct them to put equal numbers of products into each category, otherwise all of your electronic resources may become 'core'.) You could choose to protect core electronic resources from cancellation, reviewing them less frequently than those titles not central to your users. Once these rankings are established, the titles on the 'expendable' lists will be those targeted for cancellation if the need arises. Another value of the ranking process is that each subject area will be able to use this same list to consider cancellations of products in order to fund new titles. With no new funds in many library budgets, this may be the only way new electronic databases, journals and books can be acquired, and new products are still being offered regularly.

Prepare for the fallout

No matter how inclusive your process and how logical your cancellation decisions, your faculty, students and even your colleagues will protest the decisions. Because these products are so widely available, once gone they will be missed. The best way to address these concerns is to prepare a response that establishes the context for the review, discusses the review process and offers an alternative to the product that was cancelled. The selector responsible for that subject area should take the lead in handling complaints, because she knows the products serving her faculty and students, and can place cancellation decisions within the broader context of all information resources in that subject area. Users may need to learn about another product, revert to using a print resource or request the content through interlibrary loan. But, in all likelihood, the information they need remains available to them.

While canceling some electronic resources is inevitable, whether to save money or to acquire new titles, you might consider some alternatives to outright cancellation. One option is to ask your information provider whether it is able to offer pricing on a per-seat basis, if you are not already accessing the product using this model. Rarely do information providers price their products using two different models, but ask. If you are already paying based on concurrent users, you could reduce the number of seats, which should reduce your costs. Also some of us, for a number of valid reasons including interface consistency, have licensed our third-party databases primarily from one information provider, and have not revisited that decision. Comparing access models and pricing among these companies may allow you to save money without losing access to valuable content. But be sure to review your renewal notices after the first year. You may be offered an extremely low initial price in order to gain your business, but the renewal costs could increase substantially to compensate for the competitive price you were offered in the first year. Finally, if the product is not available from another provider and the content is of value to your users, you should let your information provider know that you are considering cancelling the product. It may be able to reduce the price enough to encourage you to maintain the subscription for another year. Again, watch the renewal cost, and be prepared to follow through on the cancellation if the price increase is too high relative to the value of the product.

The review process overall

Not all products are the same, and they should not be managed in the same way. For example, it does not make sense to include individual journal titles in the review process outlined above; the large number of individual titles would make the ranking process overwhelming. Subject specialists are the best people to determine the value of an individual journal title within their disciplines, because they know the literature in their field and the research strengths of your institution's faculty. The review of electronic journals will most logically be incorporated into the review of all journal titles, no matter what their format. Journal packages – consisting of journal titles from a single publisher and covering a number of different subject areas – may be licensed for multiple years at a time, and thus not fit into the review cycle for other electronic resources. Because of the complexity of these agreements, and the number of different subject areas covered by titles in these packages, they should be evaluated and new contracts negotiated by a separate committee established for just this purpose.

Other titles you may choose to exclude from an annual review process are those that you purchased outright, such as journal backfiles or digital archive collections. These titles can cost tens, if not hundreds, of thousands of dollars, and often require the purchaser to pay an annual maintenance or platform fee. Relative to the one-time cost of the product, the annual maintenance fee is usually not very high. But when all maintenance fees are combined, the total can be substantial. If your agreement permits you to host this content on a local server, and you have the server space and technical support to implement such a decision, you might choose this option. You could save the annual access fee, but then expend that saving on staff time devoted to managing these products. Consult with your computer support people to make sure this is a viable, and fiscally prudent, option.

Instituting an electronic resources review process, just one of the many activities required to manage your electronic resource portfolio, will undoubtedly be a challenge. Every student, faculty member, librarian and staff member has his/her favorite product, and believes that he or she could not accomplish their research or do their job if that product was no longer available. But in the end, no product is indispensable. If your review process is followed consistently, and that process offers ample opportunity for input from those who know your electronic resources collection best, then you will be able to defend your decisions easily. Inevitably, a user will be upset that a product has been cancelled. All subject specialists should be prepared to respond to these concerns with alternative strategies that will enable the user to find a suitable substitute.

Note

1. More information about Project COUNTER can be found at www.projectcounter.org.

6

Model licenses and license alternatives

Model licenses

Large corporate information providers and publishers have developed their own specialized electronic resource licenses, written with their company's specific needs and concerns in mind. Because so many different licenses are being used in the information marketplace, some libraries have been compelled to develop electronic resource librarian positions to negotiate and manage them all. But many smaller independent publishers, societies and non-profit organizations do not have the legal staff or licensing knowledge available in-house to create their own documents. These organizations may choose to adapt a model license. Libraries and consortia, as well as publishing consultants, have created licenses from both library and publisher perspectives. Other groups have put together licensing principles – a stated series of concerns and best practices – to guide the creation of electronic resource license agreements.

Both the library and the publishing worlds find some value in model license agreements, as demonstrated by their participation in such efforts. For companies and societies that cannot afford to hire an attorney to draft a unique contract, these licenses offer a solid framework from which to develop a customized document. Electronic resource librarians find helpful language that they can incorporate into agreements. Both groups save time. And the library community in particular uses sample agreements and statements of principles as communication tools. These public documents illustrate both subscriber and publisher needs, making both parties aware of potential areas of conflict and offering alternative language. But rarely will either a publisher or a subscriber accept a model license without some alterations. Some sample model licenses and licensing principles are available from the following organizations through their websites.

- *International Coalition of Library Consortia (ICOLC) Statement of Current Perspective and Preferred Practices for the Selection and Purchase of Electronic Information.* The ICOLC, representing library consortia around the world, has adopted this document outlining the needs and concerns of the higher education library community, as well as best practices for these organizations in licensing access to electronic resources. Available at www.library .yale.edu/consortia/statement.html.

- *Regents of the University of California/California Digital Library.* This agreement was designed to serve the needs of the Californian university system, following the principles of the ICOLC licensing statement. Available at http://cdlib.org/vendors/CDLModelLicense.rtf.

- *Council on Library Information Resources/Digital Library Federation/Liblicense Standard Agreement (CLIR/DLF).* Input from librarians, lawyers, university officials and publishers was combined to create this model agreement. Available at www.library.yale.edu/ ~llicense/modlic.shtml.

- *John Cox Associates/LicensingModels.com.* ICOLC and American Library Association licensing principles and resources available on the Liblicense website, as well as a variety of publisher licenses, were reviewed in putting together these model licenses. Available at www. johncoxassociates.com/default.asp?Page=CPD.asp.

For the purposes of this book, the sample license used as the basis for the discussion about terms and conditions was chosen from among the hundreds the author has reviewed over a six-year period. The license selected is an adaptation of one of the models available from John Cox Associates on LicensingModels.com. All of its model agreements, which it developed cooperatively with other concerned constituencies, are in the public domain and thus freely available for any publisher to adopt and modify.

License alternatives

After devoting all these pages to the electronic resource license, I am now pleased to say that electronic resource licenses may become a thing of the past. A very few publishers do not require libraries to agree to licensing terms in order to access their content. These information providers believe that copyright law is sufficient, and see no need to add further constraints on their products' use. A more likely alternative to licensing, however, is being developed under the umbrella of NISO (the National Information Standards Organization). In response to a number of concerns, including the high cost of negotiating and managing licensing agreements for both librarians and information providers, Judy Luther (Informed Strategies) and Selden Lamoureux (University of North Carolina Chapel Hill Libraries) began a public dialog about licensing alternatives. A small group of librarians and publisher representatives met in 2006 and developed the Shared E-Resource Understanding, or SERU.

SERU is not a contract; rather, it is a statement of common expectations from the perspectives of both the licensing company and the library or subscriber, and is intended to replace a legal contract. SERU does contain much of the same information as that found in our sample license; but rather than being presented as requirements, the information is presented as commonly understood principles of behavior and expectations. For example, under the 'uses' section, SERU states that US copyright law governs how the subscriber may use the product's contents. Then the document outlines, in very general terms, what misuses of the product are of concern because they can jeopardize the publisher's content and business. Neither section is the laundry list of dos and don'ts that we see in a license. The version of SERU being discussed currently (late 2007) is available at www.niso.org/committees/SERU/index.html. As the document is updated, any changes will be available from this same site.

If a specific model license, SERU or some other statement of mutually agreed-upon principles becomes the way in which publishers and libraries conduct business in the future, both parties would benefit. While not completely eliminating the need for the electronic resources librarian, such a trend would shift our focus from negotiating all agreements to negotiating only those that still require a license. We would spend the bulk of our time managing these products, as the number available will continue to grow.

7

Conclusion

Licensing, negotiating and managing electronic resources require knowledge and experience usually not associated with librarianship and until recently rarely taught in library science programs. As these resources proliferate, along with other library materials that are increasingly licensed rather than purchased, someone within the library needs to have a background in law and business, along with an understanding of libraries and their users. This book has attempted to fill the educational gap that exists between library science offerings and the business and legal knowledge necessary to become a successful electronic resources librarian.

The necessary legal knowledge includes a general background in copyright law and how that law affects the use of protected materials. While some view copyright law as limiting, licensing terms can be even more restrictive, further constraining how your faculty, staff and students can access and use electronic information sources. After learning copyright law, the electronic resources librarian should understand the language found in a standard database or electronic journal license. This includes permitted uses, prohibited uses, indemnities, warranties and jurisdiction clauses, for example. An understanding of this language is needed, because some of the requirements might not only be undesirable for your institution but may also be unenforceable.

If the terms and conditions in an electronic resource contract prove to be unacceptable to your institution, they should be negotiated. The librarian who understands the needs of the publisher, the library and the content users will be able to create a cooperative environment within which successful negotiations can occur. Approaching negotiations with a combative attitude will not encourage the product representative to work with you to resolve the concerns you may have with the license. Suggesting alternatives to replace unacceptable language is another way to approach the contract negotiation process constructively. This book has offered possible substitute language throughout, primarily in the form of the sample license.

Because their exposure throughout a university community is far-reaching and their content is interdisciplinary, electronic resources become ingrained in the research culture, making them difficult to manage or even cancel. Therefore, title cancellation or interface change decisions have to be participatory. Involving a representative group of people with broad subject expertise will help in actually making complex product decisions, as well as lending legitimacy to these decisions. These people know the literature in their fields, and will be able to consider product usage data and interface access options in order to make the best cancellation and retention decisions for your library.

Beyond all of the practical advice offered in these pages, the electronic resources librarian needs to be flexible. The way information providers and librarians interact is changing continually. If we are not licensing content, we will no doubt be working with publishers in other ways to disseminate the ever-growing body of research produced in academic institutions. Libraries benefit by having people in their institutions who are able to bridge the gap between the commercial and academic worlds, providing a conduit so that both arenas are able to accomplish their purpose – disseminating information to our users.

Appendix I
Sample license: American Society of Basketry and Knitting

THIS LICENSE IS AGREED the first day of January 2008
BETWEEN

ACME INFORMATION COMPANY, of 333 Elm Road, Somewhere, NY 11111-0000 in the State of New York in the United States of America ('the Publisher') and

LARGE STATE UNIVERSITY, 111 Main Library, Anytown, PA 15555 in the State of Pennsylvania in the United States of America ('the Subscriber')

WHEREAS the Publisher holds the rights granted under this License

AND WHEREAS the Subscriber desires to use the rights and the Publisher desires to grant to the Subscriber the license to use the rights for the Fee, subject to the terms and conditions of this License.

IT IS AGREED AS FOLLOWS:

1.   KEY DEFINITIONS

1.1   In this License, the following terms shall have the following meanings:

Authorized Users. Current members of the faculty and other staff of the Subscriber (whether on a permanent, temporary, contract or visiting basis) and individuals who are currently studying at the Subscriber's institution, who are permitted to access the Secure Network from within the Library Premises or from such other places where Authorized Users work or study (including but not limited to Authorized Users' offices and homes, halls of residence and student dormitories) and who have been issued by the Subscriber with a password or other authentication, together with other persons who are permitted to use the Subscriber's library or information service and access the Secure Network but only from computer terminals within the Library Premises.

Commercial Use. Use for the purposes of monetary reward (whether by or for the Subscriber or an Authorized User) by means of sale, resale, loan, transfer, hire or other form of exploitation of the Licensed Materials. For the avoidance of doubt, neither recovery of direct costs by the Subscriber from Authorized Users, nor use by the Subscriber or by an Authorized User of the Licensed Materials in the course of research funded by a commercial organization, is deemed to be Commercial Use.

Course Packs. A collection or compilation of materials (e.g. book chapters, journal articles) assembled by members of staff of the Subscriber for use by students in a class for the purposes of instruction.

Electronic Reserve. Electronic copies of materials (e.g. book chapters, journal articles) made and stored on the Secure Network by the Subscriber for use by students in connection with specific courses of instruction offered by the Subscriber to its students.

Fee. The Fee set out in Schedule 1 or in new Schedules to this License which may be agreed by the parties from time to time.

Library Premises. The physical premises of the library or libraries operated by the Subscriber, as specified in Schedule 2.

Licensed Materials. The electronic material as set out in Schedule 1 or in new Schedules to this License that may be agreed by the parties from time to time.

Secure Network. A network (whether a standalone network or a virtual network within the Internet) which is only accessible to Authorized Users approved by the Subscriber whose identity is authenticated at the time of log-in and periodically thereafter consistent with current best practice, and whose conduct is subject to regulation by the Subscriber.

Server. The server, either the Publisher's server or a third-party server designated by the Publisher, on which the Licensed Materials are mounted and may be accessed.

Subscription Period. That period nominally covered by the volumes and issues of the Licensed Materials listed in Schedule 1, regardless of the actual date of publication.

2.   AGREEMENT

2.1   The Publisher agrees to grant to the Subscriber the non-exclusive and non-transferable right, throughout the world, to give Authorized Users access to the Licensed Materials via a Secure Network for the purposes of research, teaching and private study, subject to the terms and conditions of this License, and the Subscriber agrees to pay the Fee.

2.2   This License shall commence at the beginning of the Subscription Period, for each of the Licensed Materials as set out in Schedule 1 or in new Schedules to this License that may be added subsequently; and shall automatically terminate at the end of the Subscription Period, unless the parties have previously agreed to renew it.

2.3   On termination of this License, the Publisher shall provide continuing access for Authorized Users to that part of the Licensed Materials which was published and paid for within the Subscription Period, either from the Server or from the archive described in 7.4 or by supplying electronic files or CD-ROMS to the Subscriber subject to payment of such fees as the parties may agree except where such termination is due to a breach of the License by the Subscriber which the Subscriber has failed to remedy as provided in 10.1.1 and 10.1.3 of this License.

3.   USAGE RIGHTS

3.1   The Subscriber, subject to clause 6 below, may:

3.1.1 Make such local electronic copies by means of caching or mirrored storage of all or part of the Licensed Materials as are necessary solely to ensure efficient use by Authorized Users;

3.1.2 Allow Authorized Users to have access to the Licensed Materials from the Server via the Secure Network;

3.1.3 Provide Authorized Users with integrated access and an integrated author, article title, abstract and keyword index to the Licensed Materials and all other similar material licensed from other publishers;

3.1.4 Provide single printed or electronic copies of single articles or chapters of the Licensed Materials at the request of individual Authorized Users;

3.1.5 Display, download or print the Licensed Materials for the purpose of internal marketing or testing or for training Authorized Users or groups of Authorized Users.

3.2 Authorized Users may, under copyright law and subject to clause 6 below:

3.2.1 Search, view, retrieve and display the Licensed Materials;

3.2.2 Electronically save individual articles, chapters or items of the Licensed Materials for personal use;

3.2.3 Print off a copy of individual articles, chapters or items of the Licensed Materials;

3.2.4 Distribute a copy of individual articles, chapters or items of the Licensed Materials in print or electronic form to other Authorized Users.

3.3 Nothing in this License shall in any way exclude, modify or affect any of the Subscriber's statutory rights under the copyright law.

4. SUPPLY OF COPIES TO OTHER LIBRARIES

4.1 The Subscriber may, subject to clause 6 below, supply to an Authorized User of another library (whether by post or fax or secure transmission, using Ariel or its equivalent, whereby the electronic file is deleted immediately after printing), for the purposes of research or private study and not for Commercial Use, a single paper copy of an electronic original of an individual document being part of the Licensed Materials.

5. COURSE PACKS AND ELECTRONIC RESERVES

5.1 The Subscriber may, subject to clause 6 below, incorporate individual articles, chapters or items of the Licensed Materials in printed Course Packs and Electronic Reserve collections for the use of Authorized Users in the course of instruction at the Subscriber's institution, but not for Commercial Use. Each such item shall carry appropriate acknowledgement of the source, listing title and author of the extract, title and author of the work, and the publisher. Copies of such items shall be deleted by the Subscriber when they are no longer used for such purpose. Course Packs in non-electronic, non-print-perceptible form, such as audio or Braille, may also be offered to Authorized Users who, in the reasonable opinion of the Subscriber, are visually impaired.

6. PROHIBITED USES

6.1 Neither the Subscriber nor Authorized Users may:

6.1.1 Remove or alter the authors' names or the Publisher's copyright notices or other means of identification or disclaimers as they appear in the Licensed Materials;

6.1.2 Systematically make print or electronic copies of multiple extracts of the Licensed Materials for any purpose other than back-up copies permitted under clause 3.1.2;

6.1.3 Mount or distribute any part of the Licensed Materials on any electronic network, including without limitation the Internet and the World Wide Web, other than the Secure Network.

6.2 The Publisher's explicit written permission must be obtained in order to:

6.2.1 Use all or any part of the Licensed Materials for any Commercial Use;

6.2.2 Systematically distribute the whole or any part of the Licensed Materials to anyone other than Authorized Users;

6.2.3 Publish, distribute or make available the Licensed Materials, works based on the Licensed Materials or works which combine them with any other material, other than as permitted in this License;

6.2.4 Alter, abridge, adapt or modify the Licensed Materials, except to the extent necessary to make them perceptible on a computer screen to Authorized Users. For the avoidance of doubt, no alteration of the words or their order is permitted.

7. PUBLISHER'S UNDERTAKINGS

7.1 THE PUBLISHER WARRANTS TO THE SUBSCRIBER THAT THE LICENSED MATERIALS USED AS CONTEMPLATED BY THIS LICENSE DO NOT INFRINGE THE COPYRIGHT OR ANY OTHER PROPRIETARY OR INTELLECTUAL PROPERTY RIGHTS OF ANY PERSON. THE PUBLISHER SHALL INDEMNIFY AND HOLD THE SUBSCRIBER HARMLESS FROM AND AGAINST ANY LOSS, DAMAGE, COSTS, LIABILITY AND EXPENSES (INCLUDING REASONABLE LEGAL AND PROFESSIONAL FEES) ARISING OUT OF ANY LEGAL ACTION TAKEN AGAINST THE SUBSCRIBER CLAIMING ACTUAL OR ALLEGED INFRINGEMENT OF

SUCH RIGHTS. THIS INDEMNITY SHALL SURVIVE THE TERMINATION OF THIS LICENSE FOR ANY REASON. THIS INDEMNITY SHALL NOT APPLY IF THE SUBSCRIBER HAS AMENDED THE LICENSED MATERIALS IN ANY WAY NOT PERMITTED BY THIS LICENSE.

7.2 The Publisher shall:

7.2.1 Make the Licensed Materials available to the Subscriber from the Server in the media, format and time schedule specified in Schedule 1. The Publisher will notify the Subscriber at least sixty (60) days in advance of any anticipated specification change applicable to the Licensed Materials. If the changes render the Licensed Materials less useful in a material respect to the Subscriber, the Subscriber may within thirty (30) days of such notice treat such changes as a breach of this License under clause 10.1.2 and 10.4;

7.2.2 Use reasonable endeavors to make available the electronic copy of each journal issue in the Licensed Materials within fifteen (15) days of publication of the printed version. In the event that for technical reasons this is not possible for any particular journal, as a matter of course, such journal shall be identified at the time of licensing, together with such reasons;

7.2.3 Provide the Subscriber, within thirty (30) days of the date of this License, with information sufficient to enable the Subscriber to access the Licensed Materials;

7.2.4 Use reasonable endeavors to ensure that the Server has adequate capacity and bandwidth to support the usage of the Subscriber at a level commensurate with the standards of availability for information services of similar scope operating via the

World Wide Web, as such standards evolve from time to time over the term of this License;

7.2.5 Use reasonable endeavors to make the Licensed Materials available to the Subscriber and to Authorized Users at all times and on a 24-hour basis, save for routine maintenance (which shall be notified to the Subscriber in advance wherever possible), and to restore access to the Licensed Materials as soon as possible in the event of an interruption or suspension of the service.

7.3 The Publisher reserves the right at any time to withdraw from the Licensed Materials any item or part of an item for which it no longer retains the right to publish, or which it has reasonable grounds to believe infringes copyright or is defamatory, obscene, unlawful or otherwise objectionable. The Publisher shall give written notice to the Subscriber of such withdrawal. If the withdrawal results in the Licensed Materials being no longer useful to the Subscriber, the Subscriber may within thirty (30) days of such notice treat such changes as a breach of this License under clause 10.1.2 and 10.4.

7.4 The Publisher undertakes to use reasonable endeavors to provide or to make arrangements for a third party to provide an archive of the Licensed Materials for the purposes of long-term preservation of the Licensed Materials, and to permit Authorized Users to access such archive after termination of this License.

7.5 Collection and analysis of data on the usage of the Licensed Materials will assist both the Publisher and the Subscriber to understand the impact of this License. The Publisher shall provide to the Subscriber or facilitate the collection and provision to the

Subscriber and the Publisher by the Subscriber of such usage data on the number of articles and of abstracts downloaded, by journal title, on an annual basis for the Publisher's and the Subscriber's private internal use only. Such usage data shall be compiled in a manner consistent with applicable privacy laws, and the anonymity of individual users and the confidentiality of their searches shall be fully protected. In the case that the Publisher assigns its rights to another party under clause 11.3, the Subscriber may at its discretion require the assignee either to keep such usage information confidential or to destroy it.

7.6 EXCEPT AS EXPRESSLY PROVIDED IN THIS LICENSE, THE PUBLISHER MAKES NO REPRESENTATIONS OR WARRANTIES OF ANY KIND, EXPRESS OR IMPLIED, INCLUDING, BUT NOT LIMITED TO, WARRANTIES OF DESIGN, ACCURACY OF THE INFORMATION CONTAINED IN THE LICENSED MATERIALS, MERCHANTABILITY OR FITNESS OF USE FOR A PARTICULAR PURPOSE. THE LICENSED MATERIALS ARE SUPPLIED 'AS IS'.

7.7 EXCEPT AS PROVIDED IN CLAUSE 7.1, UNDER NO CIRCUMSTANCES SHALL THE PUBLISHER BE LIABLE TO THE SUBSCRIBER OR ANY OTHER PERSON, INCLUDING BUT NOT LIMITED TO AUTHORIZED USERS, FOR ANY SPECIAL, EXEMPLARY, INCIDENTAL OR CONSEQUENTIAL DAMAGES OF ANY CHARACTER ARISING OUT OF THE INABILITY TO USE, OR THE USE OF, THE LICENSED MATERIALS. IRRESPECTIVE OF THE CAUSE OR FORM OF ACTION, THE PUBLISHER'S

AGGREGATE LIABILITY FOR ANY CLAIMS, LOSSES, OR DAMAGES ARISING OUT OF ANY BREACH OF THIS LICENSE SHALL IN NO CIRCUMSTANCES EXCEED THE FEE PAID BY THE SUBSCRIBER TO THE PUBLISHER UNDER THIS LICENSE IN RESPECT OF THE SUBSCRIPTION PERIOD DURING WHICH SUCH CLAIM, LOSS OR DAMAGE OCCURRED. THE FOREGOING LIMITATION OF LIABILITY AND EXCLUSION OF CERTAIN DAMAGES SHALL APPLY REGARDLESS OF THE SUCCESS OR EFFECTIVENESS OF OTHER REMEDIES. REGARDLESS OF THE CAUSE OR FORM OF ACTION, THE SUBSCRIBER MAY BRING NO ACTION ARISING FROM THIS LICENSE MORE THAN TWELVE (12) MONTHS AFTER THE CAUSE OF ACTION ARISES.

8. SUBSCRIBER'S UNDERTAKINGS

8.1 The Subscriber shall:

8.1.1 Use reasonable endeavors to ensure that all Authorized Users are appropriately notified of the importance of respecting the intellectual property rights in the Licensed Materials and of the sanctions which the Subscriber imposes for failing to do so;

8.1.2 Use reasonable endeavors to notify Authorized Users of the terms and conditions of this License and take steps to protect the Licensed Materials from unauthorized use or other breach of this License;

8.1.3 Use reasonable endeavors to monitor compliance and, immediately upon becoming aware of any unauthorized use or other breach, inform the Publisher and take all reasonable and appropriate steps, including disciplinary action, both to ensure that such activity ceases and to prevent any recurrence;

8.1.4 Provide the Publisher, within thirty (30) days of the date of this Agreement, with information sufficient to enable the Publisher to provide access to the Licensed Materials in accordance with its obligation under clause 7.2.3. Should the Subscriber make any significant change to such information, it will notify the Publisher not less than ten (10) days before the change takes effect;

8.1.5 Keep full and up-to-date records of all IP addresses and provide the Publisher with details of such additions, deletions or other alterations to such records as are necessary to enable the Publisher to provide Authorized Users with access to the Licensed Materials as contemplated by this License;

8.1.6 Use reasonable endeavors to ensure that only Authorized Users are permitted access to the Licensed Materials.

8.2 SUBJECT TO APPLICABLE LAW, THE SUBSCRIBER AGREES TO INDEMNIFY, DEFEND AND HOLD THE PUBLISHER HARMLESS FROM AND AGAINST ANY LOSS, DAMAGE, COSTS, LIABILITY AND EXPENSES (INCLUDING REASONABLE LEGAL AND PROFESSIONAL FEES) ARISING OUT OF ANY CLAIM OR LEGAL ACTION TAKEN AGAINST THE PUBLISHER RELATED TO OR IN ANY WAY CONNECTED WITH ANY USE OF THE LICENSED MATERIALS BY THE SUBSCRIBER OR AUTHORIZED USERS OR ANY FAILURE BY THE SUBSCRIBER TO PERFORM ITS OBLIGATIONS IN RELATION TO THIS LICENSE, PROVIDED THAT NOTHING IN

THIS LICENSE SHALL MAKE THE SUBSCRIBER LIABLE FOR BREACH OF THE TERMS OF THE LICENSE BY ANY AUTHORIZED USER PROVIDED THAT THE SUBSCRIBER DID NOT CAUSE, KNOWINGLY ASSIST OR CONDONE THE CONTINUATION OF SUCH BREACH TO CONTINUE AFTER BECOMING AWARE OF AN ACTUAL BREACH HAVING OCCURRED.

8.3 The Subscriber shall, in consideration for the rights granted under this License, pay the Fee within thirty (30) days of receipt of invoice and, if applicable, thirty (30) days prior to each subsequent Subscription Period and receipt of such payment shall be a condition of this License coming into effect. For the avoidance of doubt, the Fee shall be exclusive of any sales, use, value added or similar taxes and the Subscriber shall be liable for any such taxes in addition to the Fee.

9. UNDERTAKINGS BY BOTH PARTIES

9.1 Each party shall use its best endeavors to safeguard the intellectual property, confidential information and proprietary rights of the other party.

10. TERM AND TERMINATION

10.1 In addition to automatic termination (unless renewed) under clause 2.2, this License shall be terminated:

10.1.1 If the Subscriber willfully defaults in making payment of the Fee as provided in this License and fails to remedy such default within thirty (30) days of notification in writing by the Publisher;

10.1.2 If the Publisher commits a material or persistent breach of any term of this License and fails to remedy the breach (if capable of remedy) within sixty (60) days of notification in writing by the Subscriber;

10.1.3 If the Subscriber commits a willful material and persistent breach of the Publisher's copyright or other intellectual property rights or of the provisions of clause 3 in respect of usage rights or of clause 6 in respect of prohibited uses;

10.1.4 If either party becomes insolvent or becomes subject to receivership, liquidation or similar external administration.

10.2 On termination all rights and obligations of the parties automatically terminate except for obligations in respect of Licensed Materials to which access continues to be permitted as provided in clause 2.3.

10.3 On termination of this License for cause, as specified in clauses 10.1.1 and 10.1.3, the Subscriber shall immediately cease to distribute or make available the Licensed Materials to Authorized Users except as provided in clause 2.3.

10.4 On termination of this License by the Subscriber for cause, as specified in clause 10.1.2 above, the Publisher shall forthwith refund the proportion of the Fee that represents the paid but unexpired part of the Subscription Period.

11. GENERAL

11.1 This License constitutes the entire agreement of the parties and supersedes all prior communications, understandings and agreements relating to the subject matter of this License, whether oral or written.

11.2 Alterations to this License and to the Schedules to this License are only valid if they are recorded in writing and signed by both parties.

11.3 This License may not be assigned by either party to any other person or organization, nor may either party sub-contract any of its obligations, except as provided in this License in respect of and the management and operation of the Server, without the prior written consent of the other party, which consent shall not unreasonably be withheld.

11.4 If rights in all or any part of the Licensed Materials are assigned to another publisher, the Publisher shall use its best endeavors to ensure that the terms and conditions of this License are maintained.

11.5 Any notices to be served on either of the parties by the other shall be sent by prepaid recorded delivery or registered post to the address of the addressee as set out in this License or to such other address as notified by either party to the other as its address for service of notices. All such notices shall be deemed to have been received within fourteen (14) days of posting.

11.6 Neither party's delay or failure to perform any provision of this License as a result of circumstances beyond its control (including, without limitation, war, strikes, floods, governmental restrictions, power, telecommunications or Internet failures, or damage to or destruction of any network facilities) shall be deemed to be, or to give rise to, a breach of this License.

11.7 The invalidity or unenforceability of any provision of this License shall not affect the continuation or enforceability of the remainder of this License.

11.8 Either party's waiver, or failure to require performance by the other, of any provision of this License will not affect its full right to require such performance at any subsequent time, or be taken or held to be a waiver of the provision itself.

11.9 This License shall be governed by and construed in accordance with New York law; the parties irrevocably agree that any dispute arising out of or in connection with this License will be subject to and within the jurisdiction of the courts of New York.

AS WITNESS the hands of the parties the day and year below first written

FOR THE ACME INFORMATION COMPANY

Signed: _____

Name (in block capitals): _____

Date: _____

Position/title: _____

FOR LARGE STATE UNIVERSITY

Signed: _____

Name (in block capitals): _____

Date: _____

Position/title: _____

SCHEDULE 1
LICENSED MATERIALS SUBSCRIPTION PERIOD
AND ACCESS METHOD

A Schedule dated 1 January 2008 to the License dated 1 January 2008 between the Acme Information Company and Large State University.

THE LICENSED MATERIALS

Title	Subscription Period	Format	Delivery Schedule
Peer-reviewed Journals: *Transactions of the AABK* *Applied Basketry and Knitting* *Journal of Basketry and* *Knitting Safety*	2008 issues	web	15 days/ issue date
Basketry/Knitting Standards	2008 edition	web	June 2008
AABK Annual Meeting Papers (average 300 papers per year)	2008 meeting	web	July/Aug 2008
Specialty Conference Proceedings (normally 2–3 books per year)	2008 conference	web	throughout year
Textbooks (normally 1–2 per year)	2008 books	web	as published
Monographs (normally 1–2 per year)	2008 books	web	as published

Total fee for above: $2,600

ACCESS METHOD

☐ Authentication via User ID/password and IP Address

☐ Authentication via IP address

AS WITNESS the hands of the parties the day and year below first written

FOR THE ACME INFORMATION COMPANY

Signed: _____

Name (in block capitals): _____

Date: _____

Position/title: _____

FOR LARGE STATE UNIVERSITY

Signed: _____

Name (in block capitals): _____

Date: _____

Position/title: _____

SCHEDULE 2
LIBRARY PREMISES

A Schedule dated 1 January 2008 to the License dated 1 January 2008 between the Acme Information Company and Large State University.

List of addresses of the Subscriber's Library Premises, Domain Name(s) and IP addresses and/or ranges:

Class B Network: first two network numbers plus asterisks for host addresses, i.e.: 125.64.*.*

Class C network: first three network numbers plus an asterisk for host address, i.e.: 125.64.133.*

Single station: all four numbers, i.e. 125.64.133.20; or ranges, i.e. 125.64.133.20-125.64.133.40

Library name and address	Domain name(s)	IP addresses/ ranges
Main Library	lrg.edu	111.222.*.*
West Regional Library	lrg.edu	22.33.1.*
South Regional Library	lrg.edu	22.33.1.*

Network contact: Name:

Telephone: Fax: E-mail address:

AS WITNESS the hands of the parties the day and year below first written

FOR THE ACME INFORMATION COMPANY

Signed: _____

Name (in block capitals): _____

Date: _____

Position/title: _____

FOR LARGE STATE UNIVERSITY

Signed: _____

Name (in block capitals): _____

Date: _____

Position/title: _____

Appendix II
Conference on Fair Use – guidelines for educational multimedia copying limitations by media type

Motion media

Up to 10% or 3 minutes, whichever is less, of a single copyrighted motion media work.

Text material

Up to 10% or 1,000 words, whichever is less, of a single copyrighted work of text.

Text material – poems

An entire poem of less than 250 words

> but no more than three poems by one poet,
>
> or five poems by different poets from any single anthology.

In poems of greater length:

> up to 250 words
>
> but no more than three excerpts by a single poet
>
> or five excerpts by different poets from a single anthology.

Music, lyrics and music video

Up to 10% but no more than 30 seconds of music and lyrics from a single musical work.

Any alterations to a musical work shall not change the basic melody or the fundamental character of the work.

Illustrations and photographs

Reproduction or incorporation of photographs and illustrations is more difficult to define with regard to fair use because fair use usually precludes the use of an entire work.

> A photograph or illustration may be used in its entirety.
>
> No more than 5 images by an artist or photographer.
>
> Not more than 10% or 15 images, whichever is less, from a single published collected work.

Numerical data sets

Up to 10% or 2,500 fields or cell entries, whichever is less, from a database or data table. A field entry is a specific item of information, in a record of a database file. A cell entry is the intersection where a row and a column meet on a spreadsheet.

Appendix III
Institutional checklist

Authorized users

Faculty   ____

Staff   ____

Students   ____

Visiting faculty   ____

Walk-in users   ____

FTE count

Undergraduates   ____

Graduates   ____

Professional   ____

Head count   ____

Authorized sites

On campus   ____

Remote access   ____

Branch Campus 1   ____

Branch Campus 2   ____

Research lab   ____

Network information

IP addresses   _____

Proxy server address   _____

State licensing requirements

No limitation of liability   ____

Cannot indemnify third party   ____

Must have fiscal exigency escape clause   ____

Jurisdiction must be in-state   ____

No arbitration   ____

Internal licensing requirements

Interlibrary loan permission

Format permitted: Print   ____   Electronic   ____

Electronic reserves   ____

Course packs   ____

Scholarly sharing   ____

Post-cancellation access   ____

Archival access   ____

Administration

Billing contact   _____

Technical support contact   _____

References

Constitution of the United States of America (1787) The Constitution Society; available at: *www.constitution.org/constit_.htm* (accessed: 7 January 2008).

Digital Library Federation (2004) DLF Electronic Resources Management Initiative; available at: *www.diglib.org/standards/dlf-erm02.htm* (accessed: 10 January 2008).

Harper & Row v. Nation Enterprises, 471 U.S. 539 (1985).

Fisher, Roger and Ury, William (1981) *Getting to Yes: Negotiating Agreement Without Giving In*. Boston, MA: Houghton Mifflin.

Frazier, Kenneth (2001) 'The librarians' dilemma: contemplating the costs of the Big Deal', *D-Lib Magazine*, March; available at: *www.dlib.org/dlib/march01/frazier/03frazier.html* (accessed: 25 March 2008).

Phelps, S. and Lehman, J. (eds) (2004) *West's Encyclopedia of American Law*, Vols. 1–13, 2nd edn. Detroit, MI: Gale.

Index